"Waugh and Garrison treat *Montreal Main* with all the complexity that a vanguard film dealing with the relationships between men and boys deserve. They eloquently describe and analyze the film, placing it at the interstices of film aesthetics, sexual liberation history, and the larger history of representations of the desiring body. They ask how it was possible to frame the questions about men's and boys' eroticism and longing, and largely non-controversially, and they suggest why such open explorations would give way not many years later to banal and predictable plots on television police serials. At once a formal reconsideration of a lost film treasure and astute analysis of debates about intergenerational desire, *Montreal Main* is a 'must read' for film critics and historians of sexuality alike."

—*Cindy Patton, Canada Research Chair in Community, Culture and Health and Professor of Sociology, Simon Fraser University; author of* Cinematic Identities

"A passionate hybrid of theory, film criticism and social history, engaging the cutting edge of contemporary sexual politics. Waugh and Garrison brilliantly explore this forgotten gem of Canadian neo-realism, and in the process, critically revisit the turbulent riches of early seventies debates concerning the representation of intergenerational desire ... a sustained, subtle interrogation of this haunting, enigmatic masterpiece."

—*John Greyson, filmmaker*

Arsenal Pulp Press | Vancouver

MONTREAL MAIN

A QUEER FILM CLASSIC

Thomas Waugh & Jason Garrison

MONTREAL MAIN: A Queer Film Classic
Copyright © 2010 by Thomas Waugh & Jason Garrison

ARSENAL PULP PRESS
211 East Georgia Street, Suite 101
Vancouver, BC V6A 1Z6 Canada
arsenalpulp.com

The publisher gratefully acknowledges the support of the Canada Council for the Arts and the British Columbia Arts Council for its publishing program, and the Government of Canada through the Book Publishing Industry Development Program for its publishing activities.

Queer Film Classics series editors: Matthew Hays and Thomas Waugh

Cover and text design by Shyla Seller
Edited for the press by Susan Safyan
All film stills (except where indicated) © Frank Vitale

Mixed Sources
Cert no. SW-COC-001271
© 1996 FSC
FSC

Printed and bound in Canada

CANADIAN CATALOGUING IN PUBLICATION DATA

Waugh, Thomas, 1948-
      Montreal Main / Thomas Waugh and Jason Garrison.

(A queer film classic)
Includes bibliographical references and index.
Issued also in electronic format.
ISBN 978-1-55152-364-4

  1. Montreal Main (Motion picture). 2. Vitale, Frank, 1945- —Criticism
and interpretation. I. Garrison, Jason II. Title. III. Series: Queer
film classics

PN1997.M662W38 2010   791.43'72   C2010-905916-6

to the memory
of queen actor-scriptwriter-artist-poet-collaborator Peter
Brawley (1947–2006), who lived across the street and
could never get laid, and

of David Dewees:

Generations of men are like the leaves.
In winter, winds blow them down to earth,
but then, when spring season comes again,
the budding wood grows more. And so with men—
one generation grows, another dies away.

—*The Iliad*, Homer, Book VI, lines 181–185
Translation by Ian Johnston

CONTENTS

FOREWORD: The Pedophile Freeze-frame

Thomas Waugh and Jason Garrison's *Montreal Main: A Queer Film Classic* is a powerful deterritorialization, if one chooses to use a Deleuzian term, of official queer, hegemonic queer, liberal queer, or simply acceptable queer.

As Ken Plummer points out in *Telling Sexual Stories*, a story can not be told until its time comes—but what about a story that cannot be told, period, or told the way it happened? In a very significant sense, Waugh and Garrison's is a retelling of intergenerational homoerotic relationships prior to the freeze-framing of the pedophile as always abusive and exploitative.

The brilliance of the film and the power of Waugh and Garrison's "dissection," as they call it, is that it leaves the interaction between twentysomething Frank and twelve-year-old Johnny open to multiple interpretations without excluding the possibilities of erotic love and desire. It presents Frank and Johnny as relative equals in "just fooling around," not knowing what is going on, and in what their feelings for one another are.

Waugh and Garrison's presentation and analysis show how *Montreal Main* is positioned to call to task and, in a way, make the LGBTQ community accountable to two additional queer constituencies excluded by what Gilles Deleuze would call the state sedentary queer community. The state or stasis works to freeze, demarcate, territorialize, regulate, and normalize all limits and margins within its frame. The two queer constituencies are men who love boys and young people who have erotic relationships with adults.

The film is tame, understated; Frank and Johnny could be friends, hanging out as friends do, or there could be an intimacy that goes further than friendship, as Johnny's parents fear. Certainly Johnny appears to be broken-hearted when Frank honors David Sutherland's demand that he not have anything more to do with his son. The radicality of the film is how the camera interacts with Johnny. The filming techné produces, responds to, and reflects Johnny as an object of desire on screen and in the gaze of the viewer. The camera positions Johnny as *object a*: the object of desire that we seek in the other, which can never be fulfilled. In a sense, Frank is irrelevant.

Montreal Main is a work that is, itself, an *object a*, and it is precisely this that has facilitated its endurance and reemergence. At the core of *Montreal Main* is surplus meaning. What it offers the viewer is a surplus of *jouissance*—three heterosexual relationships, one gay relationship, a homoerotic friendship, and intergenerational "fooling around." The viewer is left with the remnant of unconsummated intergenerational homoerotic desire.

Waugh and Garrison's presentation of *Montreal Main* acts as what Deleuze and Félix Guattari term "the war machine" within queer film, queer politics, and queer knowledge. The war machine resists fixation and is the space of social assemblages outside of and hostile to hegemonic norms. It is what Waugh and Garrison refer to as "frontier territory." They request of LGBTQ: "Why not accept this as our task—to occupy this frontier territory and tease out its complications? Or shall we take up our distinctions in order to avoid opening a discussion? Have we said enough on the subject of intergenerational sexuality?

"Easy distinctions are had at a cheap price only for those who stand at a distance, where one can ignore their political effects."

—*Shannon Bell*

ACKNOWLEDGMENTS

Our heartfelt thanks

to Robert and Brian at Arsenal Pulp and Matt, QFC series co-editor, without whose vision and risk-taking this labor of love would not have been possible;

to trailblazers Jon, Noah, and José;

to Marcin Wisniewski and Samuel Burd, our graduate student collaborators, for research and technical and programming assistance;

to Dave Douglas and Peter Rist for their contribution to our cultural—and political—heritage in initiating the *Montreal Main* restoration;

to Frank Vitale, John Sutherland, Allan Moyle, Steve Lack, Erik Bloch, Kirwan Cox, Marielle Schouten-Levine, and Anne Henderson for their generosity with their time, networks, and memories as we researched *Montreal Main*;

to the University of Toronto Press; the National Film Board of Canada; Lois Siegel; Karen Cummings, Jake Ebert, Terre Nash, and the Peter Brawley estate; the Cinémathèque québécoise; and Cvmc.net for help with or permission to reprint certain materials in this book;

to the devoted perfectionists at Arsenal Pulp, designer Shyla Seller, copyeditor Susan Safyan, and publicist Janice Beley;

to Concordia University Faculty of Fine Arts for its generous and unfettered support of edgy research;

to Bill, Mike, John, Matt, and others unnamed for crucial love, support, and feedback during the production of this book;

and to other members of our respective support groups: Brendan, Brian, Daniel, Étienne, Ezra, Greg Y., Harvey, Jack, Jason C., Raj, Ross, Tom, Yannlemasseur, and Yuriy; Granny, Val, Colin, and Vaun.

SYNOPSIS

In his loft on "the Main" (Boulevard Saint-Laurent) in
Montreal, Frank, a twentysomethng bohemian photographer, kicks out his strung-out girlfriend Pam. On the other
side of the city, Ann and David Sutherland, a thirtysomething middle-class couple, prepare for a party to welcome
home their friend Jackie, the girlfriend of Frank's best friend
Bozo. After mock-cruising Bozo, Frank drives him to the
Sutherlands to reunite with Jackie. Although their friends
Steve and Peter find themselves excluded from the party
for being too gay, Frank and Bozo experiment with mutual
masturbation on the way. At the party, Frank wanders upstairs and comes upon long-haired twelve-year-old Johnny
Sutherland. With Ann's permission, Frank takes Johnny up
the "Mountain" (Mont Royal, a parkland hill in the city of
Montreal), and the pair warm to one another, taking photos
and playing games. That night, Frank's sleep is disturbed—
perhaps by his memories of the day. Meanwhile, Jackie nee-
dles a dismissive Bozo for commitment. Introducing Johnny
to his friends at a greasy hot dog and arcade joint, Frank gets
advice from Peter: "You can't crowd a kid," and Bozo's jealousy surfaces. Johnny's father scolds him for returning home
late. That night, Steve, Peter, and Bozo do coke and take
in the sexual sights of the lower Main, while Johnny steals
out of bed and bicycles across town. The next morning,

Bozo frightens Jackie with his misogynistic treatment of two young hitchhikers. Johnny and his pal Tony end up back in the arcade, and Steve repels an older man eyeing them, rapping about the dangers of the Main. Bozo defends Peter and Steve after a failed introduction to an offended Jackie. Frank and Johnny spend the day quietly experimenting with electricity and discussing their friendship, while the Sutherlands seem to worry. Steve raps with Johnny about his friendship with Frank. Ann vainly probes Johnny about his adult friend. Bozo and Steve cynically compare Johnny to a tabloid crime victim. The next day, Jackie breaks up with that "son of a bitch" Bozo, who, in turn, tells Steve that "Frank is fucked." A truant Johnny joins Frank and Bozo to go to a rural fair where Bozo "steals" Johnny away from Frank during the day's adventures. Returning home late, Johnny goes to sleep at his friend Tony's, and David's paternal anger explodes when he must retrieve him. On the Main, tensions between Bozo and Frank finally erupt into violence. David confronts Frank and tells him to stop seeing his son. Johnny runs away again, but Frank tells him their friendship is over, abandoning him on a backstreet. Bozo reconciles with Frank amid confusion about his own motivations. Johnny is seen back at the arcade, playing a rifle game alone.

CREDITS

Montreal Main (Boulevard Saint-Laurent Montréal)
1974, Canada
88 min.
16mm, color, sound, 1:66:1
Production Company: President Film, in cooperation with the Canadian Film Development Corporation. Video pre-shoot produced in cooperation with Vidéographe and the Canada Council.
Director: Frank Vitale
Assistant Directors: Allan Moyle and Steve Lack
Producers: Frank Vitale, Allan Moyle
Producer (video pre-shoot): Maxine McGillivray
Associate Producer: Kirwan Cox

Cast (playing themselves)
Frank Vitale, Allan Moyle, Steve Lack, John Sutherland, Peter Brawley, Ann Sutherland, David Sutherland, Jackie Holden, Pam Marchant, Anthony Booth.

Crew
Scenario: the cast, based on original story by Frank Vitale
Music: Beverly Glenn Copelann
Camera: Eric Bloch
Camera (video pre-shoot): Chris Anstead

Sound Recorder: Pedro Novak
Editor: Frank Vitale
Assistant Editor: Susan Schouten
Editors (video pre-shoot): Jon Michaelson and Roman
     Soleki

DVD release (2009), restored by Dave Douglas in
     collaboration with Peter Rist, Concordia University, and
     Audio-Visual Preservation Trust. Letterbox 1.85:1.
Distribution: Sanya Productions and Home Entertainment,
     www.montrealmain.com.
Commentary tracks by Frank Vitale, Allan Moyle, Steve
     Lack, and John Sutherland, and by Thomas Waugh.

Filmed in Montreal, Quebec, summer and autumn 1972.
Previewed at Canadian Film Symposium, Winnipeg,
     Manitoba, February 1974, and at National Film Theatre,
     Ottawa, March 3, 1974.
Premiered at "New American Filmmakers," Whitney
     Museum of American Art, New York, March 7, 1974.
Official selection of Mannheim, Locarno, London, and Los
     Angeles film festivals. Submitted and not retained for
     Canadian Film Awards.

INTRODUCTION

> You're into the kid, right? I mean, you dig the kid.
> —Steve, *Montreal Main*

This film is a kid. Or rather this is a kid film. It is a kid film in two senses: First, *Montreal Main* is a feature fiction about a love relationship between a twelve-year old boy and a twenty-five-year-old man in which the kid gradually appropriates the entire narrative and performs its parting shot.

Second, it's a "kid" film, as in, an orphan of film history, an intense but charming street urchin on the pot-holed boulevard of the *septième art*. When we say it's an orphan film, we don't intend the usual implication that its parentage is unknown, for it is very well-known indeed: director Frank Vitale and his raggedy band of McGill University refugees, bohemians, and film fanatics miraculously midwifed this low-budget independent production in the heady early years of the Canadian film industry. What we mean is more in line with the *Dictionnaire du cinéma québécois*' designation of the film as a "shooting star, a film without ancestor and without descendents" ("*une étoile filante, un film sans ancêtre et sans postérité*," Euvrard 2006, 738). While we will show that this categorical statement is not literally true, that *Montreal Main* has dozens of cousins throughout film history—both

FIGURE 1. Johnny Sutherland, production still by Frank Vitale, 1972. The kid in the "kid film."

Canadian and international, queer and non-queer, many more or less as unaffiliated as this one—we will also claim it as wondrously and uniquely rich and brave, standing alone and genealogically adrift on the boulevard, catching our eye and demanding rescue and a home.

A legendary film in some circles, though out of major circulation for decades, *Montreal Main* has been rescued—lovingly restored for DVD release by Concordia University's Dave Douglas and Peter Rist, thanks to funding from the late-lamented Audio-Visual Preservation Trust. We hope this book, which both celebrates and interrogates *Montreal*

Main's status as a queer film classic—as "queer," as "film," and as "classic"—will be part of a collective initiative to reintegrate the film as part of our heritage as film lovers, whether we are Montrealers or Canadians or erstwhile or present-day kids, queers in the expansive or narrow sense, or, above all, as citizens who champion sexual, artistic, and political freedom.

This book, like *Montreal Main*, is a collaborative project. Our book is a dialogue between two voices and two sensibilities, representing different generations and different sexual-identity monikers. We are united in our admiration for this brave "kid" but see him from different angles—political, historical, artistic, and affective. Despite our multitude of angles, we hope that our dialogue—eschewing for the most part the linear-driven argumentation of the ideal monograph and embodying sometimes complementary points of view and sometimes principled divergence—will offer a provocative starting point for the reader in his or own process, either as a longtime *Montreal Main* devotee or as your kid-like initiate. Sometimes our voices are distinct, less often merged, and we ask you, the reader, to join us in this open-ended intellectual, political, and cultural collaboration.

In Chapters One and Two, we focus on the historical context of *Montreal Main*. Situating the film clearly and imaginatively in the past, we show how this unique text is imprinted with several different force fields of the early

1970s—temporal, spatial, institutional, creative, political, and sexual. In Chapter Three, the focus is textual rather than contextual, and we follow the film through its sixteen "episodes," analyzing, probing, and questioning what is seen on the screen. This running reflection on cinematic form, along with the variables of performance, dialogue, and the world of the film as captured on celluloid, leads us to our final chapter, an essay that situates *Montreal Main* firmly both in the present of the twenty-first century and in the timeless present of film genre. Here we will introduce this orphan kid to his extended family, the thematic constellation of like-minded films, which might be called intergenerational, coming-of-age, man-boy, or boy-love films. From this context, or intertext, we will derive a polemics of sexual and cultural politics around child sexuality, intergenerational sexuality, pedophilia, and their societal regulation.[1] We will claim ourselves as the posterity of this film without posterity. In our conclusion, we will think briefly about the concept

---

1. Although the authors employ a dangerous term like "pedophilia" in the analysis, and indeed *Montreal Main* deals with pedophilia, the scope of the discussion contained in this book is limited. Unlike the term "pedophilia" itself, which maddeningly covers both tiny babies and eighteen year olds, the films in the intertext trace the experiences of boys around the age of twelve, like our protagonist Johnny at the junction between childhood and adolescence, a middle region sufficiently challenging for our purposes. We invite the readers to keep this in mind as they traverse the book.

of the term "classic" in addition to "queer," about memory and audience, and wonder who remembers this film and its cousins ... and why.

Meanwhile, the useful "extras" on the new DVD version of the film contribute as virtual appendices to our book, including an on-location interview and commentary track by the principal surviving filmmakers, Frank Vitale, Allan "Bozo" Moyle, Stephen Lack, and Johnny Sutherland.

We would like to thank these four above-named troupers for their contribution to the reinvigoration of their work more than thirty-five years after its creation, as well as Dave Douglas, Peter Rist, and the Audio-Visual Preservation Trust (a worthwhile program axed by the neo-right, culture-hating federal Conservative minority government in 2009), for their scrupulous reclamation of historical memory, and finally Arsenal Pulp Press for their risk-taking commitment to the maintenance of queer and cinematic heritage in the twenty-first century's uncertain publishing marketplace.

We dig the kid.

ONE: CONTEXT: Time and Space

Montreal Main is one of those films that I can never stop writing about, and it's been on or off one burner or another, front or back, since I first saw it when it played at its premiere at the Whitney Museum of American Art in New York City in 1974. Despite the Whitney's rubric of "New American Filmmakers Series," I think this is one of the unacknowledged masterpieces of *Canadian* independent fiction film, and of international queer cinema to boot—not that the latter concept existed in 1974. But such language must be used sparingly, for the expectations it engenders tend to pin this butterfly to the wall, to paraphrase one of Steve Lack's more memorable lines in the film. Instead, we begin by sketching the film's history.

The time

In 1972, the year *Montreal Main* was conceived of and shot, the politics of the sexual revolution, of the youth counterculture, and of nation, province, and city—all inherited from the 1960s—intersected in a momentous way. Pierre Elliott Trudeau was at the peak of his power as majority Liberal prime minister of Canada, though the slumping economy would lead to his near-defeat at re-election on October 30, just as the *Montreal Main* shoot was coming to an end. Few media pundits remembered, during that campaign, that only three years earlier, Trudeau had spearheaded the de-criminalization of sodomy in the Canadian criminal code.[2] Canadian gays and lesbians, echoing their peers around the world—most of whom did not share even the Canadians' less-than-full decriminalized status—were beginning to mobilize politically, and the Montreal "community" was doing so in its own distinct, dysfunctionally bilingual way. On the Quebec political scene, nationalist fervor was at a fever pitch following the October Crisis of 1970, a source of fascination for expatriates like director Frank Vitale. Although the 1973 Quebec provincial election returned the Liberals over-whelmingly to power in Quebec, the *indépendantiste* Parti Québécois became the official opposition, having increased its share of the popular vote to thirty percent.

The short-lived Front de libération homosexuel was started in 1972 and disbanded by August of that year. Was this Montreal group's radical mission and name inflected by their New York counterpart, the Gay Liberation Front, their Parisian precursor, the Front homosexuel d'action révolutionnaire, by Vietnamese and Algerian national liberation movements, or by Canada's own militant nationalist organization,

2. This decriminalization, effected by the Criminal Law Amendment Act, 1968–69 (or Omnibus Bill, C-150), was not full or unconditional, of course, maintaining inherited age-of-consent laws as well as sanctions on some categories of anal sex, on public sex, and on sex work—as did the 1957 British "Wolfenden report" framework on which the colonial Canadian model was based.

the Front de libération du Québec, which had fomented the "apprehended resurrection" of the October Crisis two years earlier (and who called Trudeau a *tapette* [faggot] for good measure in the process)? Most likely a combination of all three. No matter, the group disbanded that year in the face of police harassment and internal rifts. Most of the more enduring gay political action was taking place on the anglophone side of the city, at McGill University, host of already legendary monthly gay dances, and in the West End gay ghetto around Stanley Street. This commercial zone was hopping (so much so that the other momentous Montreal gay film of the early seventies, *Il était une fois dans l'Est* [*Once Upon a Time in the East*, André Brassard and Michel Tremblay, 1974], was shot in a West End club rather than in the "eastern," more francophone location that would have been more appropriate). The West End bars and saunas were full of McGill students like the *Montreal Main* characters Frank, Bozo, and Steve and flaming, artsy dropouts like Peter. The community flourished despite intermittent police harassment and "cleanup," which the civic administration unleashed seemingly at whim and which would escalate as the countdown to the 1976 Olympics gathered speed. A couple of blocks away from the most popular bars, and right next door to one of the hottest bathhouses, the radical gay-and-lesbian collective bookstore L'Androgyne had been founded in shared space with the anarchist collective Alternatives; here, Parker Tyler's pioneering compendium on gay cinema,

Screening the Sexes (1972), was on sale, along with an eclectic bilingual line of guidebooks, André Gide novels, and gay-lib manifestos.

A couple of miles to the east, there lingered a sprinkling of working-class francophone taverns on the fringes of the Main, such as the Bellevue and the Monarch (Demczuk and Remiggi, 1998). On the Main itself was Cléopâtre, the lively drag club on which *Il était une fois* was based and the center of the city's robust transgender cabaret heritage (Namaste 2005). The *Montreal Main* troupe probably hung out in the bars, but Frank and Bozo were the only ones in the circle using the newly politicized labels of sexual identity like "gay" (Peter simply calls himself a "queen").[3] Moyle's recollection of a personal basis for the film's narrative—"I was in love with you, Frank, and that was the times, you know?"—indicates not only the autobiographical dynamic of the film, but also the "bisexual chic" of a moment and milieu for whom the glitter and glam of openly bisexual rock star David Bowie was a kind of icon. (Critic Mark Finch finds the bisexual sensibility in the film "cynical," but we disagree—one must distinguish between this tender and sincere film and its cynical and volatile character Bozo [Finch 1987]). Gay, bisexual, and curious baby boomers—some perhaps not even aware

3. To alleviate confusion in talking about a fictional film in which historical figures play fictional characters with their own names, we use the characters' first names to refer to the fictional personages and the actors' surnames to refer to the historical people playing them.

that Trudeau had banished the state from their bedrooms in
1969—celebrated the lifestyle consumerism that was both
enabling and suffocating the more vanguard manifestations
of gay political mobilization, especially around such issues as
parenting and custody, anti-discrimination, censorship, police oppression, age of consent, etc. They were reaping the
whirlwind of the sexual revolution, the counterculture, Quebec laicization and modernization, and Montreal's heredi-
tary status as Canada's sin capital all at once. Within Quebec
francophone culture, distinct artistic and political discourses
around sexual diversity and identities were clamoring for legitimacy, if not authority[4] (alongside the radical feminism
that was ensuring that reproductive rights became a de facto
reality in Quebec before the other provinces). Flamboyantly
outspoken playwright Michel Tremblay was at the forefront
of the arts scene, and at least one out gay politician, Claude
Charron, sat on the Parti Québécois shadow cabinet. Together with Quebec's "live-and-let-live" heritage of Gallic
Catholicism and the Napoleonic Code, the political mobilizations around same-sex liberation that surged through
Anglo-Saxon North America seemed somehow either an
awkward import or oddly beside the point. Everyone knew
Tremblay was gay, but he did not come out officially in the

4. The French-language sitcom *Le Paradis terrestre* was yanked off
the public airwaves of Radio-Canada in 1972 because of a furor over
a minor male character seen holding hands with another man in an
elevator (Perron 2010).

media until 1975 because no one had thought to ask—and then he did so first with the Anglo media (Burnett 2010).

Little of this is explicitly visible on the screen in *Montreal Main*. In fact, as John Greyson observes, the film was "made by two bi-curious Anglo best friends, their noses pressed to the glass of Montreal's gay demi-monde, content to steam the glass but not venture within." He elaborates that Vitale not only doesn't notice the fledgling gay rights movement, but also "refuses to reference political struggles of any description that were then playing out on Montreal streets: fights around language laws, the anti-poverty activism of the time, native and immigrant rights ..." (Greyson 2009). Still, the film offers "fleeting glimpses, scraps and gestures" of a vibrant metropolis that was not only one of North America's most politically volatile but also its gayest. This context is sensed just off-screen when Frank and Bozo comment that most of their friends are gay, and when, on a nocturnal joy-ride to the lower Main, the whole gang jokes about on the omnisexual menagerie visible on the sidewalks: "doll boys," "college stars," "baby basket balls," and "picturesque chickens" are all in view through the van windows. In 1980, I wrote about the film's reflection of the anglophone gay community of the 1970s and the overlapping anglophone counterculture, casting *Montreal Main* as a vivid document of that world seen from the inside. But now I might emphasize more the degree to which it also absorbed energy from its francophone surroundings (though it is a far cry from its cotemporaneous *Les Ordres* [*Orders*, Michel Brault, 1974], another docu-fiction hybrid, focused on the October Crisis). Despite the ambiguities, duplicities, and evasions around official sexual identity in *Montreal Main*'s script, the mise-en-scène, and the credits—which perplexed me but did not dampen my ardor—I did not hesitate to assign the label "gay" to the film because of the centrality of its same-sex problematic (Waugh 1980). I saw it then as the semi-autobiographical story of an erotic relationship between two males, with a third jealous male at its triangular apex, and two flaming choristers commenting on the action from the sidelines—and much more. One of the males, as it happens, is twelve.

The question of intergenerational sexuality as it is now formulated was scarcely on the radar of early 1970s, post-Stonewall sexual politics. Despite occasional eruptions, it was most often subsumed under the categories of homosexuality and gay liberation for both the commercial and the political queer subcultures. Theorists of and spokespeople for the gay revolution were either matter-of-fact or defiant. Radical journals like *Fag Rag* (in Boston) and *The Body Politic*, the Toronto gay paper, advocated for abolition of age-of-consent laws (Jay and Young 1976). Paris's Front homosexuel d'action révolutionnaire had jumped the gun in 1971, offering a stirring manifesto by its "minors commission":

> Thus we want to destroy society's moral order,
> as we do its social order: we want to destroy

THE NOTION OF THE MINOR, for it's
a phallocratic notion of inequality. All of our
society rests on relations of inequality, "someone
has to be in charge," "everyone according to his
deserts." These are received ideas, imposed by a
minority, a class that lives by the exploitation of the
majority. WE REFUSE THE VALUES OF THE
PRIVILEGED CLASS, and the notion of the minor
that etymologically tends to reduce us to the state
of being minor, inferior, less important because we
are not yet mature and educated. WE CONSIDER
OURSELVES ALREADY AS WHOLLY ENTIRE
BEINGS with the freedoms and responsibilities
that that implies ... we represent the future. But we
don't give a damn about their future. We want to
come right away. We affirm the right to dispose of
ourselves, our right to pleasure. Opposed to our
will for emancipation, there are THE LAW, THE
FAMILY, THE MILIEU... (Front homosexual
d'action révolutionnaire 1971, 99; trans., Waugh)

In 1969 in San Francisco, Carl Wittman's *A Gay Manifesto*
included the following slightly less nuanced "Note on exploitation of children":

Kids can take care of themselves, and are sexual
beings way earlier than we'd like to admit. Those
of us who began cruising in early adolescence

know this, and we were doing the cruising, not
being debauched by dirty old men. Scandals such
as the one in Boise, Idaho—blaming a "ring" of
homosexuals for perverting their youth—are the
fabrications of press and police and politicians.
And as for child molesting, the overwhelming
amount is done by straight guys to little girls: it is
not particularly a gay problem, and is caused by
the frustrations resulting from anti-sex puritanism.
(Wittman 1969; in Jay and Young 1972, 338)

Meanwhile, two openly pedophile self-help groups
formed in the UK in 1974, the year of *Montreal Main*'s release (Weeks 1977, 227), and London's *Gay Left* magazine
followed up with at least two reasoned, nuanced, and bal-
anced analyses of the issues by decade's end (Gay Left Collective 1978; Gough 1979). The kneejerk hysteria over intergenerational and children's sexualities had not yet taken
hold. *Montreal Main* may have met with an ambivalent response from the embryonic gay media of the day, but this
was about its closeness rather than the intergenerational
relationship at its core. *The Body Politic*, which would almost
be closed down by the police and the courts five years later
for exploring the reality of man-boy love with its restrained
advocacy journalism, called the film a "real cocktease" for the
way it repressed homosexuality and left its audience hoping
that the characters "would finally come out." Moreover, the
critic Ron Dayman praised the way the "sensual though

[handwritten margin note: Yed Film Criticized for not being to explicit]

latent character of the couple's relationship comes across beautifully," and the film's recognition of their entrapment "in an ageist, homophobic world where freedom is impossible." Ultimately for Dayman, its "overwhelming message [was] the denial of the rights of children" (1974).

It is important to remember that *Montreal Main* was part of a 1970s cycle of films that profited from the collapse of censorship in the late 1960s in most western jurisdictions to explore intergenerational sexuality, children's sexuality, erotic/ gender mentorship, and coming-of-age. This cycle arguably built on the momentous postwar adaptations from France and the US that had "groomed" the "serious literature/art cinema" market—namely Peyrefitte/Delannoy's *Les amitiés particulières* (*This Special Friendship*, novel 1943/film 1964) and Nabokov/Kubrick's *Lolita* (novel 1955/ film 1962).[5] The

por) off.

---

5. We shall come back to the intertext imposed by this 1970s cycle and its political implications more fully in Chapter Four, but suffice it to mention here, just to indicate the range of the decade's works: two films by Louis Malle on the heterosexual side, *Le Souffle au coeur* (*Murmur of the Heart*) (1971) and *Pretty Baby* (1978), which opened and closed the decade with portraits of a sexually active pubescent boy and girl respectively; Pier Paolo Pasolini's *Il fiore delle mille e una notte* (*Arabian Nights*, 1974) and *Salò o le 120 giornate di Sodoma* (*Salò, or the 120 Days of Sodom*, 1975), the former's sunny but unsentimental Orientalism overturned in the latter's nightmarish and dystopian version; on the more explicit side, such films as *Le sexe des anges* (*The Sex of Angels*, 1977) by Lionel Soukaz (Dyer 1990) and *Forbidden Letters* (1976) by Artie Bressan in the Parisian queer underground and San Francisco porno scene respectively; and Claude Jutra's

most important and immediate harbinger had been Luchino
Visconti's beautiful *Morte a Venezia* (*Death in Venice*, 1971),
which came out to almost universal acclaim the year before
the Vitale group undertook their film in 1972. Vitale and the
others had seen it, and though he felt the Italian elder was
doing something entirely different (in an email to Waugh, in
2010), it is hard to look at *Montreal Main* without seeing clear
resemblances. (The Oscar-winning *Midnight Cowboy* [1969]
by the still-closeted John Schlesinger was another film on
many viewer's minds, including Vitale's, which clinched the
sense that homosexuality and homosociality, rather than
intergenerational sexuality, comprised the presiding framework for the film's 1974 constituency [Evanchuck 1974].)
As John Greyson has written, "*Montreal Main* was made in
a post-sixties bubble of semi-innocent uncertainty, where
both children and adults had rejected rigid fifties definitions
of youth sexuality and embraced the concept of children's
rights, along with civil, women's and gay rights, but still had
no definitive language for what this might mean" (Greyson
2010). The final film in this 1970s intergenerational cycle
could be a film from the early 1980s, Bressan's haunting
Abuse (1983), a rescue melodrama about a gay man rescuing
a fourteen-year-old boy from familial abuse. This film can

---

unrecognized masterpiece *Dreamspeaker* (1977), a tragic tale,
obliquely delineated, of a disturbed white boy futilely seeking refuge
with an aboriginal homosocial "family," as the other important
Canadian example (Waugh 2006).

be seen as the symbolic last utterance on the cusp of what scholar Greg Youmans calls the "sea change," an ideological shift in lesbian and gay politics and culture in the late 1970s that coincided with the inauguration of two decades of silence—many would say betrayal (Youmans 2009, 76). Our conclusion will intimate how the intertext maintained itself through the years of silence, and will provide a glimpse of its rebound in the current century, enabling new spectators of *Montreal Main* to avail themselves of a rich legacy of films of like kind, a prolific corpus that "share[s] across these thirty-five years ... an insistence on the specificity, and dignity, of their varied protagonists" (Greyson 2009).

It is all too easy to forget the rich context of the eight or so years between Stonewall and the "sea change" that helps explain now why and how *Montreal Main* was received throughout the West in such a laid-back—if not always warm and welcoming—manner. Its reception in the mid-1970s seems at worst benign and at best magically unrecognizable, as the film was poised just before both celebrity homophobe Anita Bryant's "Save Our Children" campaign and the feminist political mobilization around rape and abuse, and the imposition of an embargo of all discourse on children's sexuality and intergenerational eroticism (tentatively broken only in the twenty-first century [Angelides 2004]). Most critics, even those trying a little too hard to be gay-cool, seemed to be on the same wavelength as the filmmakers in situating Frank and Johnny's relationship on the continuum of what influential feminist anthropologist Gayle Rubin would later call "benign sexual variation" (cited by Youmans 2009, 261)—even one sympathetic critic who invoked Fritz Lang's intense child-killer lynch film *M* (1931) and Kubrick's *Lolita* as her intertext (Edwards 1974). Of the more than 100 reviews I have seen, only one stands out as the exception that proves the rule as having a heavy hand on the panic button.[6]

> A story in which a father attempts to protect his adolescent son from the advances of a panting pederast, and is made to look a villain for his pains, is not my pot of tea ... [F]oul-looking, foul-sounding, and probably even offensive to the olfactory nerve, the deviate who flaunts his oddities is not my idea of a cinematic protagonist ... the homosexual's justification of his deviation as a sexual alternative is equivalent to the comparison of an intravenous injection with a gourmet banquet. The intellectualization of the deviate's problem is nothing but a hollow and pretentious claptrap ...

6. The only other pan that could be called "vicious" was from Quebec's French-language film magazine *Séquences*, still affiliated at that time with the Catholic Church (Schupp, 1973). Schupp does not even mention the taboo sexuality intimated by the film and froths hyperbolically only against the film's improvisatory rhythm, loose structure, and "total absence of style and lamentable cinematic sense."

> To a professional person dealing with disturbed
> personalities and sexual identification crises, *Montreal
> Main* may be of great significance, but to this
> filmgoer, this bizarre circus about a "misunderstood
> minority," mounted on a rather shaky cinematic
> vehicle at that, Frank Vitale's awkwardly
> propagandistic opus is but a curiosity. (Shuster 1974)

Yet, aside from "panting pederast," even Shuster's lexicon is mostly structured by "deviate" and "homosexual" rather than "pedophile." The best of the critics recognized a film about freedom—or at least about a glimpse of freedom—even if they usually read it also as being about adults' betrayal and abandonment and a child's resistance and surrender.

This moment of benign accommodation and recognition would be brought to a screeching halt by Bryant and the right-wing feminist agenda—at opposite ends of the ideological spectrum—and the shift they signaled in both Euro-American culture and what was then increasingly called the lesbian and gay movement. Youmans refers to this latter shift as "the gay liberal turn," "the funneling and displacement of gay-liberationist, radical-feminist, and cultural-feminist energies and visions into a liberal, rights-based framework," or a "foreclosure of radical potentiality and the dawn of our current liberal impasse" (2009, 5, 18, 264)—an impasse that both paralleled and reacted to the escalation of panic and hysteria about child and intergenerational sexuality in the culture at large. One example of such panic came in 1980 and is not unrelated to our story: *Times Square*, Allan Moyle's next feature after his Montreal-produced *Rubber Gun* (1977), made with American indie financing in New York, displayed a symptomatic eruption. In an interview given in 2010, Moyle revealed that the runaway teen lesbian narrative was removed from his control in the editing phase, and the sequences of erotic interaction between the two adolescent leads, one thirteen and the other fifteen, were excised (Moyle interview, 2010).

To appreciate the modest genius of *Montreal Main* in its historical context, one must also leave the international intertext/context and come back to the film's local roots in the fledgling Canadian film industry. For these roots are also intrinsic—if indirectly so—to the glimpse of sexual freedom offered by the film. Canadian films, those from both Quebec and English Canada, were already acquiring a reputation for their "weird sex and snowshoes" (to appropriate the title of Katherine Monk's book about "all the kindly, dark, quirky and obsessive sex in Canadian films," that "revel in sexual imagery on screen," and the "twisted, perverse and generally dysfunctional sex [that] has been a part of the Canadian artistic landscape for quite some time") (Monk 2001, 119, 125). Although the eight films Monk mentions from this period are publicly funded and prize-winning big-budget features that have higher profiles than *Montreal Main*[7], they do have in common with Vitale's film what Monk would call "sexual realism"— a frankness in iconography and themes about lust, variation, alienation, initiation, cruelty, perversity, and the traumas, ecstasies, and obsessions of the body. Even the two obvious "genre" entrants in Monk's list, Cronenberg's mutant-parasite thriller *Shivers* and Kaczender's perversely sado-trans-kinky thriller *Silent Partner*, are notable for their on-location shooting style in Montreal and Toronto respectively. Significantly, only two of Monk's eight selections were National Film Board (NFB) productions (both francophone), an index of how the industry had, for better or worse, established a kind of legitimacy for a national feature film industry that could tackle "adult themes," thanks to the stimulus of the Canadian Film Development Corporation (CFDC), inaugurated in 1968. The precedent had already been established in the late sixties at the NFB for fiction features that articulated the energy and contradictions of the sexual revolution, of "hip sexual modernity,"

---

7. *Goin' Down the Road* (Don Shebib, 1970); *Mon oncle Antoine* (Claude Jutra, 1971); *The Apprenticeship of Duddy Kravitz* (Ted Kotcheff, 1974); *Shivers* (David Cronenberg, 1975); *J. A. Martin Photographe* (Jean Beaudin, 1977); *The Silent Partner* (Daryl Duke, 1978); *In Praise of Older Women* (George Kaczender, 1978); and *Surfacing* (Claude Jutra, 1981). *Antoine*, *Apprenticeship*, *Praise*, and *Surfacing* all offer themes of pubescent or teen sexual initiation and desire.

but it would fall to the indie and industrial sectors rather than the state studio to push this process further in the 1970s (Waugh 2006, 61–75). The indie sectors may well have been emerging out from under the NFB shadow in the early seventies, but it was a painful process; Vitale and his group were not the only filmmakers with their eyes on the CFDC pie who fell back on public support through NFB services or arts council startup money.

Aiming at the financial and cultural legitimacy offered by the then four-year-old CFDC in 1972, Vitale failed to access this money and legitimacy at first, and only at the end of post-production, with his very respectable film in the can, was he granted $25,000 of finishing and distribution money. At the start in 1972, Vitale's group had had to put together the project with a $10,000 Canada Council grant and the infrastructural support of Vidéographe.[8] Vitale shot his first directorial project there on the still innovative Sony half-inch Portapak technology. This project, *Hitch-Hiking*, a forty-three-minute first-person docu-fiction released earlier

---

8. The involvement of Vidéographe— a downtown, storefront, predominantly francophone video cooperative—suggests the incestuous relationship the NFB had with the entire Quebec film scene: initiated as an offshoot of the Board's "Société nouvelle" program, the French wing of its influential experimental community-empowerment initiative, "Challenge for Change," Vidéographe was fast becoming an independent artist-run cooperative, which cut its apron strings to the NFB in 1973.

in 1972, was a trial experiment with autobiographical improvisation style and discreet sexual ambiguity, as well as with
spatial articulations. The artist records himself caught up in
the cross-border expressways and rail networks of Quebec,
Ontario, and New York State in a way analogous to *Montreal
Main*'s inextricable attachment to the streetscapes of Montreal. Vitale had been a frequent border crosser over the
previous years, maintaining roots in Montreal and career
hopes in New York at the same time, so the work is clearly personal—all the more so since it anticipated *Montreal
Main* with its overwhelming homosocial framework and
coy homoerotic plot twist in one episode around a seductive driver.

Vitale clearly had feature stars in his eyes, and *Hitch-
Hiking*, showing it could be done, led directly to the use
of the co-op's resources to produce the video "pre-shoot"
for *Montreal Main* that same year. Ironically, the pre-shoot
crew turned out to be bigger than the crew for the eventual
16mm shoot.[9] The *Montreal Main* video pre-shoot gave the
troupe's improvisational ensemble method its baptism by
fire and produced the working script that would be followed

---

9. The other small contribution of Challenge for Change to the
emergence of proto-queer filmmaking, other than two very oblique
feminist documentaries, one in each language about "alternative
families," was the infrastructural support it gave Harry Sutherland
as he developed what I have called the first Canadian gay-lib
documentary *Truxx* in 1977 (Waugh 1981).

FIGURE 2. Vitale in *Hitch-Hiking*. Video still.

more or less faithfully—though with greater discretion and ambiguity, as we shall see—when the 16mm shoot happened later that same fall (the wrap took place the day before the first snowfall of the season).

What was the magic ingredient in this cultural-economic context, with its labyrinthine funding process and Kafka-esque distribution reality, which led to a tendency toward "sexual realism" in film—with *Montreal Main* retroactively looking like the flag bearer? How did the sexual revolution leave an imprint on the fits and starts of the Canadian cinema of the 1970s in a way that arguably failed to leave its mark in the Hollywood mainstream or even the US indie scene?

Canadian cinephiles' openness to the influence of European art cinema was one factor, perhaps, but even more important was the funding agencies' arm's-length relationships with filmmakers, from the CFDC on down, including within the essential institutions of peer juries and directors' programming committees at the Canada Council and the National Film Board, respectively. Furthermore, Canada's three metropolitan cultural scenes (Toronto, Montreal, and Vancouver), together representing more than half of the Canadian population, harbored not only its intellectual and artistic life but also its radical sexual identity subcultures, which tended to infiltrate cultural industries and thus facilitated screen cultures of tolerance and diversity. In short, all of these factors seem to have allowed sexual radicalism to percolate on the arts scene, in cahoots with the lingering counterculture (albeit pictured in *Rubber Gun* as a fatigued, cocaine-addled rump) and radical feminism. The marginality of English-Canadian cinema doomed it to all-but-invisibility—but this meant it was under the radar of parliamentarians and not frightening the horses or other gatekeepers. The time was ripe for *Montreal Main*.

The place

> Among the penny arcades and the dime shows,
> attic above the dark racked secondhand stores
> its number; neighbour to cubicles in heat,

> hashjoints, vodvils, poolrooms—the scruffed doors
> the derelict swings, the cop on the corner knows—
> —from A.M. Klein, "Librairie Delorme"

The place was Montreal, a fertile crucible in the 1960s and 1970s for the emergence of New Wave cinemas and sexualities—and at the same time the object of the cinematic gaze. *Montreal Main* shows this par excellence. Its title notwithstanding, its story and characters do not obey Aristotle's prescription for unity of place. Rather, this movie spans six different worlds—six different localities operating as narrative matrices—sometimes encompassing these worlds and sometimes oscillating back and forth among them. Each world nourishes and regulates its own specific sexual culture, and it is from the encounters between them that the film's artistic vision springs, both grounded and volatile, classical and audacious.

The Main is the axis at the center of the film's grid of universes, but Boulevard Saint-Laurent itself contains two worlds. The "upper Main," stretching from the east–west rue Sherbrooke artery all the way north to the Canadian Pacific railway tracks, borders the then working-class and soon-to-gentrify Plateau Mont-Royal, where the *pure laine* (francophone proletariat) mingled with and worked alongside, or for, wave after wave of immigrants for whom the boulevard was the fabled "street of dreams." Before moving to the suburbs, the Jewish waves of Plateau homesteaders—immortalized by

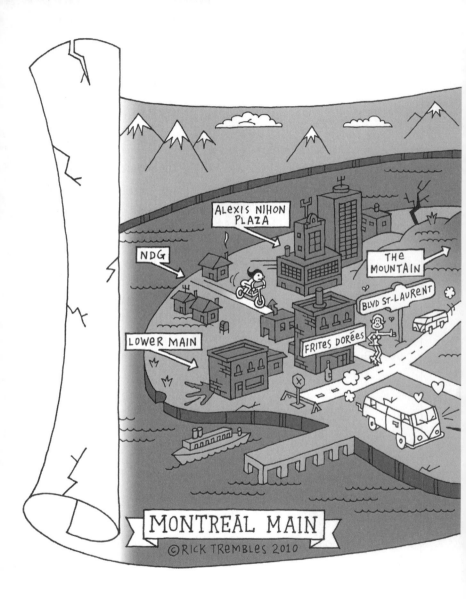

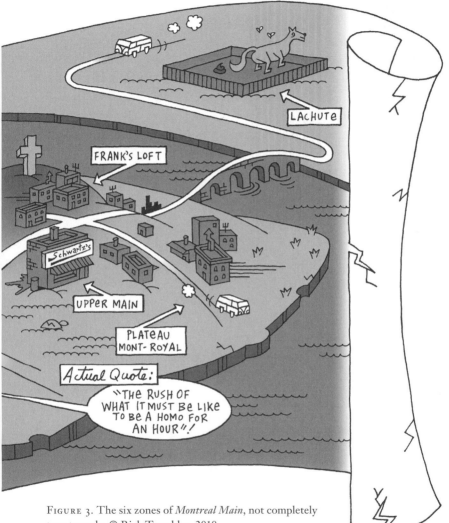

Figure 3. The six zones of *Montreal Main*, not completely true to scale. © Rick Trembles, 2010.

authors from A.M. Klein and Mordecai Richler to Leonard Cohen—left the neighborhood many distinctive landmarks and spaces. Several of these are celebrated in the film, from Schwartz's Hebrew Delicatessen to the now-abandoned garment factories whose sunny lofts Frank and his bohemian cohort were colonizing in the early seventies. As for the lower Main, which stretches downhill from Sherbrooke to Chinatown, if Frank and his friends were not garbed in thrift-store finery and driving a van whose windshield wipers don't work, one might get the sense that they are slumming when they descend the hill, literally, to hang out at Silver's Frites dorées. There they fraternize with the demimonde of prostitutes, johns, pimps, tourists, outcasts, drunks, queers, drag queens, suburban juvenile refugees, and down-on-their-lucks who hung out in the arcades, fast food joints, and clubs of the red light district. Here the lower Main crossed the city's other main east–west thoroughfare, the glittering shopping and night-life epicenter, rue Sainte-Catherine, thus configuring at the crossroads what Steve calls "the tiled urinal of Babylon." Less colorfully, one critic called this area the "tenderloin haven" (Shuster 1973), and others constructed it as a combination of Times Square and Sunset Strip. If the upper Main signified for Vitale and crew the world of relationships and urban multicultural heritage—and, as he put it in a 2009 interview, "a timeless backwater of communal dinners, art openings and parties" (2009)—the lower Main meant the charms of grunge and erotic temptation.

FIGURE 4. The lower Main. DVD still.

Several other geographical referents also shape the spatial imaginary of the film, each inhabited by its own coefficient sexual culture:

The Mountain. For some, this towering urban park is an elegant sylvan refuge and source of civic pride (it was designed by landscape architect Frederick Olmsted, who also designed New York's Central Park), but for sexual minorities it was an outlaw underground space of non-consumerized and non-productive[10] sexual freedom (Allen 1998). The Mountain had already been immortalized by founding Montreal queer

10. To use George Bataille's concept of a sexuality not determined

cineaste Claude Jutra, who had *À tout prendre*'s (*All Things Considered*, 1963) closet-y protagonist and his girlfriend attacked by a *Scorpio Rising*-style biker in a nightmare sequence unfolding on the snowy promenade (Kenneth Anger, 1964). It would also return to the screen in the next decade thanks to Denys Arcand's *Le déclin de l'empire américain* (*Decline of the American Empire*, 1986), whose gay art-historian character, Claude, compulsively returns to the Mountain's summer pathways "like a cat in heat" (Waugh 2006). Frank and Johnny's adventure in Parc Mont-Royal is the idyllic five-minute centerpiece of their movie; this is the site of the artist's photographic representation of the kid. This dynamic of queer subject and erotic object I have elsewhere situated at the center of the narrative construction of the gay male subject in twentieth-century queer cinema (Waugh 1993). The idyll is also the occasion for non-hierarchical child-like play, literally with fire, and a bucolic stroll through the autumn foliage—all tinged with the metaphoric resonance of erotic encounter. Poet A.M. Klein, raised four blocks east of Vitale's loft (who died the year of the *Montreal Main* shoot), had also reflected on the spatial geography of the metropolis and, like Vitale, had repeatedly looked to the Mountain for its mysterious sacral function: "In layers of mountains the history of mankind,/and in Mount Royal/which daily in a

---

by economic or familial instrumentality, as developed by Champagne (1995).

FIGURE 5. Frank and Johnny descend the wild side of the Mountain, DVD still.

streetcar I surround/my youth, my childhood—/the pissa-bed dandelion, the coolie acorn,/green prickly husk of chest-nut beneath mat of grass—/O all the amber afternoons/are still to be found" (Klein 1990, 698).

The Mall. The then state-of-the-art Place Alexis-Nihon was erected hubristically on top of the terminus of the glitzy new Métro, built for Expo 67 in the development frenzy of the 1960s, poised on the border between the downtown and the anglophone suburbs to the west. With its palatial atrium and vertiginous escalators, girded by more conventional shop windows of shoe stores, department stores, and ice-cream parlors, it markets the dream of conventional hetero-con-jugality. Naturally, the Mall is the recipient of Steve's more astutely analytic and Beatles-riffing monologues:

> All the lovely people, I do wonder where you all
> came from. Probably the same lettuce leaf and
> supermarkets that I did, eh ... Some kind of syndrome
> like that, reproductive syndrome, to the elements
> of reality, blah, blah, blah. There was a man getting
> stoned right on tea, right there smack dab in the
> middle of Babylonian America. I do declare, I believe
> this is the Alexis Nihon Plaza. We ain't never had it
> so good. But the towers get higher and higher, and I
> get higher with the towers.

The Suburb. Notre-Dame-de-Grâce—or NDG, for the characters of the film (and all Montrealers)—is the shady and laid-back neighborhood of single-family dwellings that the hip middle-class Sutherlands have decided is ideal for bringing up their only son. Their brick house with adjoining garage is the site of nuclear family values, of well-orches-trated group breakfasts and strict bedtimes, of the patina of 1970s chic, and of girlfriends who have prim hairdos and expectations of relationships. African masks adorn the walls, but the master bedroom dresser drawer contains a Royal Bank of Canada credit card.

The Hinterland. Rustic, rural Lachute lies northwest of

the Island of Montreal on the Ottawa River, and its live-stock auction-cum-farmers' market stands in for the *pure laine* francophone hinterland of Frank and Johnny's Anglo world. This is a kind of heterotopia, the "other place,"[11] a non-urban space of idyllic refuge or cathartic self-discovery or pastoral breathing-room, where impassive farmers bid on castrated horses and then sing folk medleys in the van on the way back to civilization. The getaway detour to this non-urban space has a charged but ambiguous relationship to the rest of the film. Just before making *Montreal Main*, Vitale had produced, in collaboration with Moyle, two works that reflected his ethnographic fascination with Quebec culture: a luminous and observant black-and-white documentary on East End Montreal's country music scene, *Country Music Montreal* (1971), resonant with the male homosocial com-munity that he would affirm in subsequent works, and an exhibition/performance week at one of the hip new artist-run spaces, Véhicule, devoted to the pickled heart of Quebec saint Frère André. His devotion had inspired the building of the Oratoire St-Joseph, the shrine that towers over the city and symbolizes the French-Canadian *terroir*'s heritage of faith and sanctity, as well as what seems to Anglo outsiders the inscrutable exoticism of French-Canadian culture. Vitale

---

11. I am relying on Michel Foucault's concept (Foucault 1986), as I develop it in its application to Canadian queer narratives in *The Romance of Transgression in Canada* (2006, 98–145).

FIGURE 6. Homosociality and an ethnographic eye in *Country Music Montreal* (1971). DVD still.

was not the first Plateau Mont-Royal anglophone to brood over the cryptic cultural environment surrounding him and its cultural and spiritual roots: Klein had also mused on the Oratoire and the "cripples" healed by the saint's intervention—not without outsider envy.

The Volkswagen van, which ferries Frank, Bozo, Johnny, and, to a lesser extent, Steve and Peter back and forth among these six universes, is arguably an onscreen world of its own—all the more so since Vitale would often tell interviewers how it had died for good the day after the wrap. It is the site of aborted desire, of misogynist acting-out, of hinterland folk music, endless relationship talk, quasi-ethnographic voyeurism, and of Johnny's blissful slumber on his mentor's lap as they drive home from Lachute.

The characters of the film inhabit these six or seven worlds unevenly, straddling or even suspended between them, between fringe and center, tradition and revolt, intersecting with the sexual subcultures proper to each. But this suspension is precarious and impermanent, as is made clear in the film's dénouement with Frank trapped immobile in his loft and Johnny marooned in the back alleys of the Plateau and staking claims in the arcades of the Lower Main.

Critics acknowledged almost without exception the "realistic," "naturalistic," and/or "authentic" presence of the city as a major character in *Montreal Main* and commended Vitale's accomplished interweaving of story and place. They were prompted by his judiciously chosen and intriguing title but also by his textured urban aesthetic based on cinematographer Eric Bloch's unerringly evocative close-up style, his eye for both detail and the backdrop landscape of façade, *ruelle* (alleyway), or street corner.

What does it mean for the question of realist recognition and authenticity of place to enter into a film's reception? Different things from different vantage points, of course. The three arguably most influential American critical voices—those of the *New York Times*, *TIME*, and *Variety*, all apparently either stuck in the Expo 67 mythology of that gleaming modern metropolis with the underground city and European *joie de vivre*, or shifting their pedophobe panic into the discourse of urban critique, all read decrepitude into the film's construction of place. Referencing the Lower Main alone, they passed on to their readers the film's delivery of "the sleazy, Bohemian areas of a Montreal far removed from the tourist's itinerary" (Weiler 1974), the "infamous lower St. Lawrence Boulevard, a run-down, neon-lit zone inhabited by winos, homosexuals and loft dwellers" (James 1974), and, most dramatically, Vitale's success "in making Montreal (one of Canadian's loveliest cities) about as appealing as [Brooklyn's notorious African-American slum] Bedford-Stuyvesant" (Robe 1974). They were outdone, however, by Seymour Stern from *Film Culture*, the New York bible of the avant-garde, whose vocabulary included not only "slum," but also "cesspool," "dilapidation," "hellish," and "panoramic acidic social decay" (1979).

But unlike the Americans, Canadian critics, especially Montrealers, more or less resisted this narrative of urban decay. They approached the film, if not always within the framework of national or civic boosterism, invariably with great empathy for Vitale and Bloch's affectionate and discerning insider ethnographic eye for the habitats of queens, winos, folksingers and working-class tenants. In short, they got it. They understood the way the city spaces inform

identities, characters, relationships, and desires in front of
Vitale's lens (Euvrard 1974). Two local student reviewers
were especially charmed; one "liked the familiarity, the intimacy projected in such scenes as Schwartz's Smoked Meat
[*sic*], Frites dorées, and Montreal's particular juxtaposition
of streets, tenements, and the corner grocery store. I liked
the perception of body movements, speech patterns, focuses
on details that are peculiar only to the senses of those of
the Montreal culture" (Somers 1974). The other reviewer
was equally mythopoeic of the Main setting, and was so em-
pathetic to the film's intergenerational queer narrative that
he clearly implied personal identification (Rubin 1974). *La
Presse*'s Luc Perreault—perhaps the most influential reviewer
er in Quebec at the time, and for that reason worth quoting here at length—incorporated a snide dig at earlier Anglo
Montreal filmmakers in his rhapsodization of this first "perfectly authentic" anglophone film shot in Quebec (without
papering over the cracks in the film or its urban subject), and
talked back to *Variety* in the process:

> "The Main" is not, strictly speaking, the main
> character of this film but she acts as a symbol to
> underline the contract in a city like Montreal
> between what corresponds geographically to two
> perfectly defined sectors, east and west. "The Main"
> is this street, St. Laurent Street [*sic*], which cuts
> Montreal in two, this street of a thousand contrasts,

cosmopolitan, with its little shops, its "*clochards*
[tramps]," its dubious cabarets, in short this street
where everything plays out in a kind of chiaroscuro,
where good and evil find themselves tightly bound
and confused so well that it is impossible to trace
a precise border on the level of people's behavior
between what is acceptable in the eyes of the
upholders of traditional morality and what can seem
to deviate from the habitual norms of a society
like ours. The Main is, in summary, a no-man's
land, the realm of deviants, the domain of mutants.
Frank and Johnnie [*sic*] represent perfect examples
of this abnormal milieu ... [*Variety*'s comment] is a
beautiful compliment for the director in the sense
that he has perfectly integrated the natural settings
made available to him and used them as expressive
elements. It was time one stopped identifying
Montreal with its skyscrapers and showed its alleys as
they are, not as film sets but as *lived spaces*. (Perreault
1974; trans. and emphasis, Waugh 2010)

The pleasure of recognizing "lived spaces" is crucial to
Canadian/Québécois cinema on the whole—or that of any
"minor" cinema in every sense of filmic marginality and deterritorialization that has been extrapolated from Deleuze's
concept of minor literature (Deleuze and Guattari, 1986
[1975]; White, 2008; Rodowick, 1997). In the 1970s, the
falsification of Canadian landscapes by runaway Hollywood

productions began in earnest, and the situation was exacer-
bated later in the decade under the notorious CFDC frameworks of co-productions and tax shelters. Inconsequential
de facto American and European films like *Agency* (George
Kaczender, 1980), *Once Upon a Time in America* (Sergio Le-
one, 1984), and *Hold-Up* (Alexandre Arcady, 1985) symptomatized the hijacking of lived spaces and voiding them
of both inhabitants and meaning. They emptied them also
of the atmosphere of loss and volatility, of the immanence
that resonates from Vitale's sense of his urban landscape,
wherein, for example, the scars of living history such as the
October Crisis were still in the process of healing.

That said, one other great Quebec queer film about the
Main was made and released at the same time, *Il était une
fois dans l'Est*. However, instead of dealing with Vitale's anglophone bohemia, Brassard and Tremblay conjured up
the francophone world of glitteringly tacky transvestite
clubs and greasy spoons as well as the working-class apart-
ments of the Plateau. Like Vitale's, Tremblay's world also
organized into neighborhood matrices, a reflex of the authenticity in his artistic procedures. The question remains
how Vitale, a Montrealer for only a decade at the time of his
film's completion, could successfully create a narrative universe so authentically anchored in lived spaces and pregnant
neighborhoods, arguably even matching native sons Tremblay and Brassard in his appropriation of local cultural and
sexual geographies and their attached narrative and sexual

imaginaries. The answer may well lie not only in his insider ethnographic eye and heart and loins, but also in the brilliant way he was seconded by native stock, the ensemble of talent and guts he enabled, cultivated, and marshaled—as we shall see in the next chapter.

TWO: CONTEXT: People and Films

"Questions for Bozo"

while every day must bring its increase,
and to the actors their obvious movements,
your people and officers direct our action.
hey, darlin' when were you where it was?
never for very long, to wake up early and
the day and interest, after all.
who is this great man of endurance?
when his night is still some rosy mystery?
who did last till dawn anyway?
all of our fools
all of our clowns
all our pretenders.
—Peter Brawley

That *Montreal Main* was a collective effort is not only amply visible on the screen and in the credits (despite the maintenance of the hierarchical "director" credit for Vitale) but this was also mentioned by almost all critics, even if only in passing. Rising to the occasion of the fertile confluence of time and place that we have explored in the previous chapter, the film's creative team was an ensemble of scriptwriting, performing, technical, musical, fundraising, and administrative talents, both amateur and professional. It inhabited an artistic milieu energized by baby boomer entitlement and ambition, New Left social awareness, and that countercultural hybrid of irreverence, narcissism, and dope, all tempered by late 1960s/early '70s cinephilia in large doses. Montreal, still clinging for a few more years to its claim as the Canadian cultural capital—between Expo 67 and the 1976 Olympics—honed a bold generational cusp, a kind of tipping point in which its vibrant institutional and cultural infrastructures all converged: from the National Film Board (NFB) to the Canadian Broadcasting Corporation (CBC) to the Canadian Film Development Corporation to its four universities; from the independent art scene to the bilingual literary and theatrical scenes; from the legendary nightlife and erotic entertainment sector to the jazz and music milieu; from a strong union movement to a vibrant and street life of demonstrations and other political theater (Vitale filmed a huge St. Jean Baptiste celebration for *Country Music Montreal*). The tension between nationalist resentment and aspiration on the francophone side and New Left countercultural energy on the anglophone side—nourished by the large influx of draft dodgers and other American expatriates since the 1960s[12], especially visible in the film milieu—were

12. Vitale was not technically a draft dodger; in an email he told me that he received deferral as a student and obtained landed immigrant status right after graduation from Montreal's McGill University in 1967. *Montreal Main*'s associate producer Kirwan Cox, however, had emigrated in protest to McGill and Montreal from Baltimore in the

also part of the formula. Federal funding thrown lavishly at the province after the October Crisis did no harm: in addition to Canada Council, CBC, and NFB/Vidéographe infrastructural support, the Vitale group used monies from "Opportunities for Youth" (Human Resources Development) and Health and Welfare's "Local Initiatives Program." They benefited from connections at both a nonprofit producer's consortium (Association coopérative de productions audio-visuels—ACPAV for short—founded in 1971 with a commitment to *auteur* cinema and still thriving four decades later), and a commercial exploitation house, Cinépix[13], which employed the penniless American as an editor, allowed him to edit *Montreal Main* at night, and would eventually produce his venture into commercial features, *East End Hustle* (1976). At the other end of the cultural gamut, Vitale and Steve Lack exhibited at Véhicule Gallery, one of a whole

1960s and renounced his American citizenship, embracing Canadian citizenship, ironically at the exact moment of the October Crisis. He became a mainstay of the indie Canadian film scene in both Montreal and Toronto in the early 1970s.

13. Cinépix, a distribution firm turned production house, was headed up by John Dunning and André Link. It had been behind the maple-syrup porn wave of the late 1960s and early '70s, as well as sympathetic patrons of such novitiate directors as Ivan Reitman and David Cronenberg. They would make a killing in the next few years with their low-budget hit dominatrix trilogy *Ilsa: She-Wolf of the SS* (Don Edmonds, 1975), *Ilsa, Harem-Keeper of the Oil Sheiks* (Edmonds, 1976), and *Ilsa, Tigress of Siberia* (Jean LaFleur, 1977).

network of federally and provincially funded artist-run centers that were springing up like mushrooms at the time.

Crew

The people

The above "perfect storm" of institutional, economic, and demographic convergence notwithstanding, it is appropriate to pause and focus on the major contributors to *Montreal Main*. This is all the more apt since this "autodocumentary" (Michaelson 1974, 39) deployed not only non-professional actors (with one exception) but also the performers' actual identities and names and even living spaces; it built, moreover, on their scriptwriting and improvisational skills as applied to their own lives and on the internal strengths and vulnerabilities these bring out (the video pre-shoot had deployed fictional names and spaces but the 16mm had wisely shifted to the semi-documentary mode). The film's self-referential elements were fully acknowledged in the discussions around the film's release and thereafter. Moyle, for example, referred to *Main* as "built around a plot that actually really happened," and Vitale called it "an experience that I had some basis in, that I had been through, whether exactly or to some extent ..." (Michaelson 1974, 4, 13).

Director

Frank Vitale was born in 1945 to a Lebanese-Italian-American family with lower-middle-class entrepreneurial aspirations in Jacksonville, Florida and was always referred to as an American in the press despite his almost fifteen years of residence in Montreal. Beginning as a McGill science student in 1963, he was soon bitten by the film bug—like so many baby-boomer cinephiles. Montreal was a movie-mad metropolis that had been welcoming the cinema of the world to its annual "Festival International du film de Montréal" since 1960; after Expo 67, nearly a decade ensued before the festival craze started up again in 1976, but a robust art-house and repertory cinema culture replaced it. This cinephile momentum was indissociable from Quebec's *Révolution tranquille* (Quiet Revolution), with its processes of laicization, urbanization, modernization, and the general craving for the outside world that had swept the province in the post-war era. The accompanying dissolution of the province's draconian film censorship regime very early in the 1960s was also an essential part of the picture: the shift from a jurisdiction that lopped off fourteen minutes from *Hiroshima mon amour* (Alain Resnais, 1959) in 1960 to the only one in Canada that dared show *Salò* (Pier Paolo Pasolini, 1975) and *In the Realm of the Senses* (Nagisa Oshima, 1976) in the mid-seventies was nothing short of radical[14] (Véronneau 1988). After spending three years going back and forth between Montreal and

14. Under Quebec's notoriously liberal film classification body, *Montreal Main* and *Rubber Gun* were both rated as "13+ *étude de moeurs*" (study of manners). Hence fourteen-year-old Johnny was able to attend the screening with his pals; meanwhile, *East End Hustle*, a film that added violence and frank nudity to the mix of taboo eroticism, got the 16+ *érotisme* classification.

New York trying to break through as a freelance filmmaker in the Big Apple (and being credited as "hippie" in two New York features by John Avildsen, *Joe* [1970], where he was "unit manager," and *Cry Uncle* [1971], where he was "associate producer"), Vitale soon came back to Montreal ("where my friends were," he recalled in a 2010 email to the author) and became integrated as a hustler and aspiring filmmaker into the local film community.

In the early 1970s, determined film fanatics could break into 16mm independent filmmaking, and Vitale and his friends performed their own version of "the boys-will-be-boys hubristic drive to 'make a movie' at any cost" (Greyson, 2009). Together with Moyle in 1971, Vitale put together his thirty-eight-minute documentary called *Country Music Montreal*, which incorporated an appearance by Johnny Cash, and which the CBC would broadcast on its "Canadian Film Makers" Sunday-afternoon slot in early 1974 (later rebroadcast by the New York PBS affiliate WNET). Vitale made another prize-winning short, *The Metropolis Organism*, in 1974, a campy treatment of the biological nature of cities, a theme jibing resoundingly with his cotemporaneous portrait of the titular city in *Montreal Main*.

Meanwhile, Vitale got involved with Vidéographe, his anglophone cultural background apparently creating no hurdles in this famously francophone and ardently *indépendantiste* artistic and political community. In contrast to the English wing of Challenge for Change, Vidéographe was a supportive forum for young cinephiles striving to express themselves in the still innovative portable video medium (at least three other star feature directors of Quebec cinema emerged from this scene—Charles Binamé, Robert Favreau, and, most famously, Pierre Falardeau). No doubt Vitale's dark, brooding, bearded Afro look and his American openness to Quebec endeared him to the Vidéographe crowd, who were, recalled Vitale in 2010, always more reserved with English Canadians. While with Vidéographe, he brought out his first artistic production, the medium-length videotape *Hitch-Hiking*, which he shot in first-person one-person-crew diary style. This experiment, as we have seen, led straight into the video pre-shoot for *Montreal Main* in 1972, shot by collaborator Eric Bloch, a graduate from Loyola College's pioneering communication arts program. The pre-shoot was an invaluable opportunity to hone the script, with its mix of key expository dialogue and more general improvisatory hooks and set-ups, as well as fine-tune performances, settings, and characters—not to mention sanitize, as we shall see.

Editing and post-production kept the crew busy for most of 1973, along with final fundraising for the new feature. After winter previews at a Winnipeg symposium on the "crisis" in Canadian cinema and at special venues in Ottawa and Toronto, the official premiere of *Montreal Main* took place at the Whitney Museum in New York in March 1974, where it enjoyed a full week's run. Thereafter, the distribution and release for the film, both theatrical and in festivals and on campuses, along with final fundraising, threatened to become almost a full-time occupation for the rest of the year. The Canadian theatrical premiere was in Vancouver, British Columbia, in April, and the film was soon greeted with rave reviews in the dailies as well as general interest newsmagazines like *Maclean's*, film magazines like *Cinema Canada*, and hippie weeklies like the *Georgia Straight*.

Montreal Main was also well covered by the Toronto gay press; it had immediately hit what one might call the "homintern gaydar." Screenings took place as early as May 1974 for the University of Michigan-Ann Arbor gay group and at the San Francisco Art Institute, where it was presciently paired with another inventive city film, Fred Halsted's art porn classic *LA Plays Itself!* (1972). Two years later, *Montreal Main* definitively entered the canon of "gay cinema" with its inclusion in the series "Homosexuality in the Movies" at Concordia University's Conservatoire d'art cinématographique, alongside such films as *Les amitiés particulières*, *Death in Venice*, and *Fellini Satyricon* (Federico Fellini, 1969). The following year it featured prominently in a series called "The Celluloid Closet: Homsexuality in the Movies," at Los Angeles's American Film Institute Theatre, a festival inspired by Vito Russo's still-in-the-pipeline epochal book of the same title (due out in 1981 but at this point still a touring clips lecture). Two years later, *Main* showed up again in Montreal's first queer-conceived festival, "La semaine du cinéma gai Montréal 1980," brought into relief by works by Lionel Soukaz and Kenneth Anger, as well as Rosa von Praunheim's 1979 *Army of Lovers or Revolt of the Perverts.* (The latter offered a thematic tie-in, a portrait of the American gay-lib scene that scandalized left and right alike by juxtaposing the proto-NAMBLA "Boston Boise Committee" with gay Nazis, all interwoven with explicit first-person authorial fucking.) By 1982, *Montreal Main* had made it to the mother of all proto-queer fests, the San Francisco International Lesbian and Gay Film Festival, where it rubbed elbows again with films by Kenneth Anger and von Praunheim, plus a teen lesbian feature by an obscure ex-Canadian, *Times Square* (Allan Moyle, 1980). A canon had been carved out, and Frank and Johnny were part of it.

Canons are one thing, theatrical runs are another—and the former don't pay the rent. By 1977, *Main*'s non-theatrical career turned out to be the pattern for the US (one night in a summer festival at Manhattan's Carnegie Hall Cinema, and one week at the Orson Welles art house in the upstate Massachusetts college-town/queer haven of Northampton, and that was it!). The Montreal first run hadn't happened until October, at the Élysée, an art-house duplex just steps from the Main (where Jodorowsky's *Sacred Mountain* [1973] was screening in the adjacent hall). That fall the film was also shown at the Mannheim, Los Angeles, Locarno, and London, UK, film festivals, which must have seemed some kind of consolation. *Montreal Main*'s Toronto run, a three-day setdown at a repertory house, did not take place until May 1975.

By then, Vitale had already shot his next directing-script-writing feature project, *East End Hustle*, a quasi-feminist, gritty urban thriller featuring tough prostitutes and corrupt pimps and cops ("Cindy was a hooker trapped in the *East End Hustle*. Now she's getting revenge on those who treated her like dirt," promised the poster). *Hustle* was produced by Vitale's friends at Cinépix, funded within the still new CFDC infrastructure, and sewn up with the new industrial skills that he had acquired first in New York and now with his Montreal circle. A slightly wobbly but competent genre property, featuring two of Quebec's up-and-coming leading ladies Andrée Pelletier and Anne-Marie Provencher, *Hustle* certainly fit the CFDC agenda.

In 1976, maintaining his skills as a cinematographer—and in a "you-scratch-my-back-I'll scratch-yours" swap with Moyle—Vitale shot much of the *Montreal Main* group's final collaborative feature project, *Rubber Gun*. This low-budget improvisational yarn, overlaid with more queer, druggie countercultural gab and a heist-genre narrative, was directed by Moyle. But the group disintegrated soon thereafter, and Vitale, Moyle, and Lack all ended up in the US by the end of 1978, apparently burnt out by the intensity of artisanal directing, producing, and fundraising in the Canadian film scene. At the same time, Vitale was attracted to the buzz and momentum that *Rubber Gun* had generated in 1977 festivals

in New York and Locarno and with its April 1978 week-
long New York run. Familial obligations were also a factor:
Vitale's mother had died unexpectedly, and, shortly after
the release of *Rubber Gun*, Vitale was already married and
living in upstate New York, looking after his younger siblings. This was a dramatic conversion, recalled Moyle, from
a supercool, LSD-popping film fanatic to a stable family guy
(Moyle 2010). His more than three-decades-long career as
prize-winning corporate filmmaker for the American NGO
The March of Dimes, based in New York City—with continuous teaching and production projects on the side—was
already underway.

Vitale was always candid in interviews and publicity material, then and now, about his stake in *Montreal Main*—sur-
prisingly so, given the personal risk and potential contro-
versy involved. Coolly nonplussed by the inevitable personal
questions, even the most intrusive ones, he always spoke
from the heart without the predictable disavowals, as if to
challenge interviewers and readers to draw whatever conclusions they desired, all the while avoiding the categorical
or definitive implication in the story of Frank and Johnny.
Typical comments might have seemed disappointingly eva-
sive to gay-lib interlocutors, but now seem refreshingly and
prophetically proto-queer almost four decades later:

> Homosexuality is something I think about. My
> best friend is a man and I am on the periphery of

the homosexual element in Montreal. But I was
raised as a heterosexual and I would be afraid to
be a homosexual. I am in a gray area between the
two. The fact that the film is about a problem that
is real to me was a source of energy. It made it
worthwhile to do. It makes the point that there is no
sharp division between the two poles of sexuality …
Sex is more a source of pleasure and emotional or
intellectual satisfaction, so the sex of the partner isn't
so important. (Gorrie 1974)

In another interview the same year, he responded to a
journalist's probing of whether he felt "weird" talking to
strangers who'd seen the insides of his head and heart:

That's the way I do things … In a sense [the film's]
a public confession … But it's just an art style, that's
all I can say about it … it's what I think I should be
doing, for some reason … and it doesn't bother me,
in fact I get a certain amount of cathartic feeling
out of exposing myself. Maybe being brought up
Catholic, brought up with the idea of original sin, I
had a lot of things to hide for a long time, parts of my
personality … so this is the way I get them out …

Like in this film politically, I'm propagandizing
for the gray area between homosexuality and
heterosexuality. I'm saying that there is such an area
and it's as real as anything else … Things aren't so

black and white that you can say this is homosexual
and that is heterosexual … I've never been very into
politics, but to me, this film is a piece of political
propaganda … The energy in the film, for a large
part, results from a sort of sexual conflict, where I'm
not too clear about my own sexuality. I'm definitely
not slanted toward being a complete homosexual. My
background, my upbringing, probably makes me very
afraid of it. (Maler 1974)

Later, to the same interviewer, Vitale candidly mulled over
translating some of his personal fantasies to the screen, even
violent sexual fantasies, and linked them to the artist's social
responsibility for honesty in his interactions with his audience: hearing this, one wonders about the graphic scenes in
East End Hustle, then in pre-production—especially one particularly vicious sexual assault of the heroine Cindy—which
corroborate the sense in *Montreal Main* of the nakedness of
the authorial psyche.

Allan "Bozo" Moyle was born in 1947 in an aluminum
town in northern Quebec, a scion of a family of engineers,
and moved to Montreal's suburban West Island as a teen,
where he developed an interest in theater. He met his "best
friend" Vitale, as well as Stephen Lack and several others
of the extended group at McGill, in the mid- to late-1960s.
A thin, clean-shaven jitterer with intense eyes and a receding hairline, Moyle joined Vitale in his efforts to break into

the New York film industry, and shared the credits with him on *Country Music Montreal.* Moyle not only co-starred in *Montreal Main*'s video pre-shoot and final version but also shared the scriptwriting credit, a perfect foil for the other lead characters. On a roll after the film's release in March 1974, Moyle extended his collaboration with Vitale that fall through credits as associate producer, production manager, co-writer and leading man in *East End Hustle.* In this quirky genre picture, he again plays a "straight man" foil for a more colorful subcultural ensemble, as the boyfriend of the film's heroine, Cindy. The casting agents brought into being by the growing CFDC took notice of his acting promise and secured him for a further memorable role in a Canadian feature, as a supporting character in the classic Toronto gay feature *Outrageous!* (Richard Benner, 1977). The latter capitalized fully on Moyle's onscreen psychotic edge and constructed him as a refugee from psychiatry, with thick, runny eyeliner and delusions about being pursued by Chairman Mao's Red Guards. Immediately after the *Hustle* shoot, Moyle starred in the Winnipeg indie feature *The Mourning Suit* (Leonard Yakir, 1975) as another straight young leading man, this time a North End Jewish musician contemplating his roots: after this film, he vowed never to act again. Soon Moyle rushed back east and moved up to the director's chair for the group's next creation, *Rubber Gun*, shot at the end of 1974 and start of 1975. In this "sequel" to *Montreal Main*, Moyle co-starred again with Lack in another homosocial

FIGURE 7. Lack cruises Moyle in *Rubber Gun*, production still, c. 1975.
© Lois Siegel Productions

duo, but this time one consummated sexually and therefore more unambiguously queer than the bromance in *Montreal Main*. A variation of his "Bozo" character from *Montreal Main*, though perhaps without the edge, Moyle's character is a naïve McGill graduate student in the social sciences writing his thesis. Picked up by the brazen Lack, he is soon researching the drug-subcultural communal "family" he has thereby discovered. The Moyle roles in *Hustle* and *Gun* are similar, featuring, among other things, ample erotic performances showcasing his taut, slim, nude body (the *Montreal Main* pre-shoot offered a similar nude scene).

Moyle is now best known as the director of the teen-genre hit *Pump up the Volume* (1990) and the Michael Jackson TV-biopic *Man in the Mirror* (2004). However, Moyle has secured one additional berth in queer film history with *Times Square*, which was a staple of the burgeoning lesbian-and-gay festival scene of the early 1980s despite its official "flop" status and disastrous run-in with censorious producers. He would also return to Canada with a well-received regional women's coming-of-age melodrama, *New Waterford Girl* (1999). Vitale and Moyle drifted apart after their departure for the US in 1978, life somehow mimicking the artful parting of *Montreal Main*. As Vitale remembered it with thirty years' hindsight,

> [T]he only real incident [in the film] was the breakup
> of Bozo and Frank as friends. It became part of the

story as it was actually happening at the time. Bozo
and I had a very close friendship for a number of
years before the film. During the film we began
drifting apart. It was a beautiful friendship and I
loved him very much, though I wasn't aware of it
at the time. I eventually got married and raised two
terrific children ... When I saw [*Pump Up the Volume*]
I saw Bozo's heart and mind on the screen. (Vitale
2009)

The former best buddies' meetings to do the commentary
track for the DVD release of *Montreal Main* and a Calgary
Cinematheque revival of both *Main* and *Gun* in 2008 were
their first meetings in decades.

Johnny Sutherland, born in 1958, was thirteen when recruited to play the taciturn long-haired, doe-eyed, long-
legged but diminutive twelve-year-old co-star of *Montreal
Main*. The filmmakers had not been able to persuade the
university professor father of an original real-life "Johnny,"
whom Vitale had been fascinated with from afar, to allow his
participation in the film and were feeling the pressure of the
last stages of casting. Despite a radio ad and fifteen tryouts,
and after lengthy unsuccessful auditions they leapt at the
boy-come-lately. Running out of time and energy, they also
snagged Johnny's real-life parents David and Ann Sutherland (1938–2009), a thirtysomething jazz musician and psy-
chologist respectively, to play his fictional mother and father

as part of the package. In an interview with Jon Michaelson in 1974, the director described the casting process:

> Frank Vitale: "I went to all these schools, all these sixth- and seventh-grade classes, gym classes, everything. I went to the parents, sent them all the script, wrote them letters, visited them, gave them the script, then called them up: and they said—"Well, thank you very much, but the kid's going away for the summer." Or something like that. I saw about a thousand kids."

> Jon Michaelson: "Out of these he found about four or five who would've been good or at least suitable, but the parents refused. (This process took about two and a half months of intensive search, contact, and follow-up work.) Finally an ad on CFCF-TV's "Movie Matinee" program brought results: about seventy five phone calls from excited parents, fifty of whom were told to send pictures in: Vitale saw about fifteen of these boys, when a friend of his brought a friend of hers over: she had a son and Johnny Sutherland (one of the last boys to be seen) proved to be what Vitale was looking for." (Michaelson 1974, 11)

Steve Lack remembers thinking at the time, "The kid's Sophia Loren. Frank found him worth staring at. The kid's together. He's a bright kid. He knows a lot." John Greyson

FIGURE 8. David and Johnny Sutherland. Production still, 1972.

adds, "Johnny is nothing short of a revelation, holding the screen with a fawn-like calm that is as mesmerizing in its own way as Björn Andrésen's rendition of Tadzio in *Death in Venice*" (Greyson 2009). Sutherland's own memories of the summer pre-shoot and the autumn 16mm shoot and finally the exhibition of the film are not very detailed or precise. An occasional anecdote, however, fleshes out the narrative of a casual, trusting, and playful artistic relationship with his adult co-filmmakers, and an overall lack of interest in exactly what would derive from the disconnected and no doubt monotonous shooting episodes first on video and then on film throughout the last half of 1972. (Johnny was the only performer to be paid, so that he would have an incentive to keep showing up.) The adult Johnny, comfortably heterosexual, scarcely comments on the risky narrative hook of his child-hood fame, but jokingly wonders whether it was his virtuoso nocturnal bicycle scene that would impel him to a career as a bicycle racer as a young adult, a career that eventually segued into retraining as a massage therapist. Sutherland's parents, Ann and David, were essential to the film's success with their understated performances. Ann exploited her quiet shrink-ish watchfulness and provided a visual echo of her son (with her long straight brown hair and owl-like gaze). David, a smoker with a bushy 1970s Afro and mutton chops, performed a more scripted role with a convincing blank tenseness that explodes when he fiercely slaps his defiant son at the violent climax of the film.

Stephen Lack delivered what was for many the most charismatic and memorable performance in *Montreal Main*, with his scene-stealing shtick as the motormouth queer scion of well-to-do Montreal Anglo Jewry (he even dons a yarmulke at one point to complement an otherwise very queer scarf and metallic vest outfit). A handsome curly-haired brunette with intense green eyes and acne-scarred skin, Lack mediates between his tense friends Bozo and Frank, whom he met at McGill in the 1960s, and between Frank and Johnny, and plays a chorus role with his nonstop commentary on the action. One reviewer called him the real star of the film (Rubin [1974] was right in a way, since Stephen certainly has more lines than the introverts Frank and Johnny combined).

His second role in *Rubber Gun*, this time the lead, essentially reprised the same seductive character (for which he received a best actor nomination from the Canadian Oscars, the Genies). Like Moyle, he too was noticed by the agencies, and was soon cast in several key CFDC productions of the early 1980s, most notably in David Cronenberg's *Scanners* (1981), where he was finally punished for his mouth by having his brain explode. Already a serious visual artist at the time of the *Montreal Main* shoot (his work can be glimpsed in the background at least once), he displayed much more of it in *Rubber Gun*, where his character is a committed painter who hard-heartedly continues with palette and canvas after his buddies have been busted. By the end of the 1970s, Lack was settled as a successful painter with wife and offspring on the Lower East Side of Manhattan, according to publicity profilers, though by other accounts this "strange conversion" (Moyle 2010) did not mean full abandonment of his queer real-life persona.

Peter Brawley (1947–2006) characterized himself as "the only queen around here" in the "greasy kid stuff" making-up sequence of *Montreal Main*. This is not inaccurate if the applicable definition of queen is a flamboyantly histrionic and effeminate genderfuck-leaning performer of everyday life—especially when high. This stocky, furry, reddish-blond, speaking in a epicene singsong drone, excelled in his supporting role as the queer commentator in *Main*. From a working-class background, he may have lacked Lack's sexual confidence in real life and "could never get laid" (Moyle 2010), but on screen it was different. His photogenic qualities are aptly summed up by Lack on the DVD commentary track:

> Peter has got to be one of the most brilliant, camera-friendly, and super-indefinable characters ever. Every time that he was in front of the camera, Allan, Frank, in both films that we did, both felt that they weren't getting anything out of him. And it wasn't until they looked at the rushes, or saw it in context, that they realized that he gave them so much more than they asked for. Every time. We aren't talking about once, twice, maybe, maybe. Every time. "Peter, Peter, give us more." And then they'd look. I mean, you don't have to give a lot when the camera is crawling all over your pores.

In *Rubber Gun*, his role would acquire even more weight—his character is betrayed and busted in the poignant dénouement of the narrative, and he delivers a distinguished performance despite being overshadowed by Lack's bravura. In one striking scene, the pair perform an over-the-top riff on *Montreal Main*'s pedophile theme, watching kids playing street hockey through a chain-link fence and sportscasting their erotic attraction: "I wonder if their cocks are just big or do they have hard-ons ... and then there's Adonis in the red ..."

FIGURE 9. Peter Brawley in makeup, *Montreal Main*. DVD still.

Brawley took on a vignette role with only a line or two in one scene of *East End Hustle* as a flamboyant dope-enabling "harem eunuch" for the coven of prostitutes from which the heroine has escaped. In an instance of life imitating art, the real-life Brawley was busted trying to import a suitcase full of hashish from India and spent the premiere of *Gun* in jail (Massé-Connolly 1978). Along with the three Sutherlands, Brawley was the only member of the troupe to keep his roots in Montreal and was the only one to stay on the Main; he became a mainstay of the parallel arts scene on the Plateau and returned to school at Concordia to finish graduate work in Art Education in 1997. Brawley died of cardiovascular problems at the age of fifty-nine. (Lack's online elegy attributed his health problems in all likelihood to "some excessive skiing on a mirror somewhere way back" ["Peter Brawley" (blog obituary) 2006].)

Other creative contributors to the ensemble achievement must also be acknowledged if only in passing. Eric Bloch, a shaggy-haired Scandinavian cinematographer, fresh out of one of Canada's earliest film production programs at Loyola College (later Concordia), joined the project cold for the video pre-shoot. Given a certain amount of freedom by Vitale to develop his own aesthetic with his minimal crew, Bloch made an important contribution to the close-up style that is a hallmark of the film, and many critics commented on its crispness and sensuality. Bloch's brief collaboration with Vitale was an exceptional departure in a career of commercial and commissioned work, as well as undeveloped projects later on in the Montreal cinema and television scene.

Kirwan Cox, associate producer, was known in Canadian film circles as a nationalist film activist and journalist (for *Cinema Canada*, among other forums) and advocate for documentary filmmaking. Cox had just produced for the NFB and his own company the prize-winning compilation documentary on the pre-history of Canadian film, *Dreamland: A History of Early Canadian Movies 1895–1939*, released the same year as *Montreal Main*. While engaged with the fundraising for *Montreal Main*, Cox was based in Toronto running the indie co-op Canadian Filmmakers Distribution Centre and commuting to Montreal to teach Canadian cin-

FIGURE 10. Eric Bloch with Vitale during video pre-shoot. Production still, summer 1972.

ema at McGill, where he was plugged into the John Grierson-Vitale nexus that was transforming English Montreal filmmaking.[15]

Susan Schouten (1945–1995), assistant editor, was a teacher in the Loyola program and a New Left feminist documentarist in her own right as well as pal of the Vitale group from McGill, where she was doing her doctorate. Her

15. John Grierson was the fiery and opinionated Scot who pioneered documentary cinema in the UK, founded the National Film Board of Canada, and by extension the Canadian cinema *tout court*, in 1939. He came back to teach at McGill for a year or so before his 1972 death and shaped a whole new generation of aspiring Canadian filmmakers, including many names on the *Montreal Main* credits.

role in *Montreal Main*, judging from post-release interviews, was more important in the project than the run-of-the-mill assistant editor. Vitale and Moyle corroborate by calling her "a central moving force" on their commentary track. Influenced by her McGill associate John Grierson (who got a "thank you" credit on *Country Music Montreal*), she was working simultaneously on her own prize-winning NFB documentary short as director and editor about her elderly mentor, Grierson, *The Working Class on Film*, released in 1975.

Beverly Glenn-Copeland (also sometimes spelled Co-pelann), a deep-voiced African-Canadian blues singer, came late to the project and provided two songs "When the Snow Flies" and "Who Do You Think You Are?" As mood or thematic interludes, layered in true seventies fashion, these songs add a "velvety vocal ache and queer urgency" to the film (Greyson 2010), a distinctive sensibility, cited by many critics. It was an expensive addition since Vitale remembers paying her most of the finishing money accorded guiltily during post-production by the CFDC. The singer is still active, now a male performer based in Toronto under the name of B. Glenn-Copeland.

Jackie Holden, the only professional performer in the film, had a background in theater; long-haired in the video pre-shoot, she sported a Jane-Fonda-in-*Klute* pixie cut in the final product. Famous for saying "insinuate" twice in her confrontation with Steve and Peter, and "supercilious" twice in her improvised breakup scene with Bozo, she left town the day after the wrap, and never appeared in another film. An occasional reviewer praised her performance, but not a single member of the troupe remembers where they found her or where she went.

Pam Marchant, another member of the Vitale circle (another of his exes), provided a small but memorable vignette as Frank's strung-out ex in glittery makeup and tie-dyed shirt. She would also have a role in *Rubber Gun*, slightly more substantial but less inclined to steal every scene she was in with her over-the-top stringing-out of a line. Marchant would later move to the US, marry, and study jewelry design. She is currently working in organic farming.

That most of the key players in the production were males is not beside the point. The community so intricately fleshed out behind the camera and on the screen is profoundly homosocial. The eloquent themes of male community torn apart by its rivalries over both women and boys and its competition with the hetero-nuclear family for control are not unconnected to currents of backlash misogyny and the "narcissism that typifies many collectively produced buddy movies" (Greyson 2009) that were common in the early 1970s. The backlash undercurrent was perhaps connected also to the simultaneous emergence of militant feminist filmmaking—of which the presence of future Studio D director-editor Anne Henderson as Frank's jilted girlfriend in the video pre-shoot is a reminder. Most symptomatic—

and most conspicuous to my students decades later—is the scene where the stressed-out Bozo screams "You scum!" with startling vociferousness and conviction at two young blonde teenybopper hitchhikers. But it was not invisible at the time either, and several critics commented on it (Stoller 1974). Homosocial narratives were not always able to detach themselves from the masculinist currents within the culture at large, and often unquestioningly incorporated eruptions such as Bozo's. Still, the strong non-sexist vignettes by Ann Sutherland and Marchant provide a strong counterbalance to Holden's cloyingly conventional nest-featherer persona.

To dwell on the nature of individual contributions is neither an auteurist's side trip, a publicist's wet dream, nor a trivial "whatever-became-of" gloss on the film. The foregoing group portrait of the key human links in the creative chain that produced *Montreal Main* is based on a conviction that the alchemy of people coming together at a particular time and in a particular place is essential to an understanding of the production of cinema, the most collaborative of the arts, and in particular a magical almost unexplainable distillation like *Montreal Main*. This intimate fresco details a milieu, as well as the melodramas many of the filmmakers had lived and were reliving in front of and behind the camera.

In 1978, with the major players except Brawley and the Sutherlands relocated to the US, and with *Rubber Gun* embarked on its commercial career, a *Cinema Canada* writer eloquently mourned the passing of an era: "Once upon a time,

FIGURE 11. "The group" (Left to right: Moyle, photographer Vitale, Lack, unidentified bearded figure, hatted Brawley). Production still by Vitale, ca. 1975.

in Montreal, there was a group of people who carved out their own physical and psychological space and then made films about it all. *Montreal Main* began the story, and *The Rubber Gun* completes it. The people have split, the curtain has come down. And Montreal is the poorer for it" (Massé-Connolly, 1978).

The films
Films about youth—alienated, bored, pregnant, marginal,

misunderstood, dropout, queer, crazy, nationalist, hippie, protesting, and horny—were the internationally recognized specialty of Canadian cinemas in the 1960s and '70s, both English and French, inside and apart from the NFB, and fiction and documentary. In comparison to Hollywood films that sold to youth (*Gidget Goes Hawaiian*, 1961; *Beach Blanket Bingo*, 1965; *American Graffiti* and *The Exorcist*, both 1973), Canadian films were authentically and insightfully *about* them as well as made *with* them and talking *to* them. *Montreal Main* belongs fully to a list that spans from *Nobody Waved Goodbye* (Don Owen, 1964) to *Outrageous!* (Richard Benner, 1977), from *Le Chat dans le sac* (Gilles Groulx, 1963) to *Les vrais perdants* (André Melançon, 1978), and includes the earnestly pedagogical George Kaczender-directed dramatic shorts from the NFB in the 1960s about anxious teen dropouts and their pregnant girlfriends. It is also connected to the proto-queer masterpiece from Toronto from a decade earlier, *Winter Kept Us Warm* (David Secter, 1965), which, like its 1970s Montreal analogue, is about young baby boomers discovering deeply buried feelings and about romantic-friendship triangles rent by jealousy and sabotage (Waugh 2006). Vitale's scenes of miscommunication between child and parent, often between mother and son, of inarticulate fumblings between adolescent or twentysomething peers, are standard tropes of all these alienated-youth films—and his dope scenes seem to be straight out of Claude Jutra's indulgent rebel-teen docudrama *Wow!* (1969).

FIGURE 12. The sexual revolution meets John Grierson: homosocial teen hash in Claude Jutra's *Wow!* (1969). Courtesy The National Film Board of Canada.

Film scholar Peter Harcourt links most of the classic youth films cited above to another Canadian tradition of artisanal, personal cinema features (Harcourt 1977). His work on *Montreal Main* did an excellent job of situating *Montreal Main* within this current:

> In the early 1960s, films grew out of personal
> enthusiasms. Canadians wanted to make movies
> about their own lives and they wanted to make
> feature films. At the Film Board, both *Le Chat dans le
> sac* (1964)and *Nobody Waved Goodbye* (1964) emerged
> from intended shorts; while outside the Board, films
> such as *Seul ou avec d'autres* (1962), *The Bitter Ash*

(1963), *À tout prendre* (1963) and *Winter Kept Us Warm* (1965) were stitched together from whatever scraps of financing the filmmakers could assemble ...

[T]here is still an underground Canadian cinema—little films made on small budgets out of individual passions ... These films have received limited exposure, carrying on the tradition of a distinguished but invisible cinema—an artisanal cinema always searching for self-definition ...

[I]n 1974, *Montreal Main* grew out of this cottage industry tradition ... Conceived by Frank Vitale but collectively directed, scripted and enacted, the film takes us into areas where we had never been before and where, to this day, some of us may not wish to go. Furthermore, as in the foundation films of the 1960s, as if to valorize their true-to-life dimension, the names of the characters retain the names of the actors. (Harcourt 2002)

The key films of the 1970s, within this tradition of "small" artisanal youth films like *Montreal Main*, increasingly gravitated around youth countercultural types (like Frank, Bozo, and gang), whether on the documentary side as in Allen King's *Come on Children* (1973) or on the fiction side as in *Outrageous!*, both of which scrutinized the heritage of the 1960s. Others continued the tradition of focusing on middle-class kids from the suburbs searching for themselves, like the cast of Don Shebib's 1971 *Rip-Off* (and like *Main*'s Johnny). Many of these, as Harcourt indicates, shared *Montreal Main*'s hybrid artisanal "true-to-life dimension" as improvised or docu-fictions, dating back at least to Claude Jutra's *À tout prendre*. The latter had been a similarly scraped-together autobiographical fiction that shared both Vitale's aesthetic strategies, his theme of taboo sexualities (an interracial heterosexual romance that ends in an abortion), and his Montreal locations and real-life character names. A few cultured local critics mentioned this precursor, and Vitale was also aware of Jutra's *Wow!*, a similarly inspired NFB feature that offered a select group of teenagers the opportunity to stage their fantasies before the indulgent director and lavish NFB crew and setup. The Anglo-Canadian director most often on the tongues of critics in 1974, however, was Allan King, whose quasi-dramatized *vérité* documentary, *A Married Couple*, about yuppie baby boomers and their toddler son traversing relationship hell, had created an international sensation in 1969. *Rose's House*, an NFB short feature from "Challenge for Change" that starred director Clay Borris's own mother as a boarding-house matron living in Toronto's working-class Cabbagetown district, was released in 1977. What we have already called the Canadian penchant for "sexual realism" was inseparable from the artisanal youth current, the iconoclasm of the Pill generation converging with the social-work heritage of Griersonian documentary in the Canadian imaginary.

American filmmakers were also an important part of *Montreal Main*'s intertext. The most prominent influence was Paul Morrissey, another inventor of artisanal docu-fiction. His trilogy *Flesh* (1968), *Trash* (1970), and *Heat* (1972), exploiting Andy Warhol's name and Joe Dallesandro's body, had established precedents for tacky glamour and gritty eroticism that Vitale would perhaps wisely tone down in his Canadian variation of the Factory's counterculture improv formula. Other south-of-the-border entrants in the genre of hybrid docu-fiction built on late-1960s material such as John Cassavetes' dissections of middle-class masculinity, Shirley Clarke's probings of urban minority subcultures, and Jim McBride's *faux-vérité* mockumentary *David Holzman's Diary* (1967). Later came Robert Kramer's undervalued *Milestones* (1975), more politicized as well as more prophetically and inclusively queer than some of its 1960s forebears.[16] The British contingent of filmmakers had also been fertile, with Ken Loach and Peter Watson at the head and Tony Garnett and queer Jack Hazan following up. As for the French, they had virtually invented the genre with the prototype 16mm equipment in the late 1950s, thanks to pioneer ethnographer

---

16. Kramer was veteran of the sixties radical documentary collective "Newsreel," and moved into the hybrid fiction formula in the seventies.

Jean Rouch (*Moi un noir* [*Black Like Me*], 1958). Finally, the Cubans and the Chileans (during the latter's brief three-year window of political and artistic freedom, 1970–73) had developed their own unique docu-fiction hybrids in *La primera carga al machete* (*First Charge of the Machete*, Manuel Octavio Gomez, 1969) and *La tierra prometida* (*The Promised Land*, Miguel Littin, 1971), which significantly were not about baby boomer relationships and sexual identities but considered geopolitical history and the wretched of the earth.

The point of this list-making is not to drown the reader in cinephilic erudition but rather to demonstrate that Vitale and company were part of an international New Wave cycle that celebrated the still new but mature 16mm lightweight sync-sound equipment in the intimate (mostly color) observation of alternative and emergent relationships, identities, demographics, and politics. This cycle harnessed the creative energy of the collaborative process and non-professional actors, re-imagining first-person cinemas and either countercultural worlds or critiques of mainstream worlds. Canadian entries had pride of place, with their understated and anxious narratives of young people coping with society. And Canadians' flair for "meandering plots that are as keen to explore the rabbit holes as they are to stick to the main road," for collapsing the line between "dramatic invention and documentary observation" (Greyson 2010), was the perfect vehicle for exploring this way of imagining and understanding. It is this flair that is evoked by Moyle's astute observation on the DVD's commentary soundtrack that *Montreal Main*'s open-ended *diminuendo* dénouement was not "a mad scene," but "just a slow Canadian fadeout."

The problem of distribution remained the unsolvable challenge for the Canadian films in this wave. Though the NFB valiantly maintained its 16mm parallel distribution wing for another decade and often included indie work for its community exhibitors and collections, edgy feature works like *Montreal Main* were left out in the cold, and festivals (especially the embryonic pre-1980 lesbian and gay screenings circuit), *cinematheques*, and campus screenings had to take up the slack. Vitale snagged three distributors, respectively Roninfilm (New York) for the American market, Toronto's New Cinema for English Canada, and Montreal's Faroun Films, which took on Quebec and world sales, bringing out a French-subtitled version called *Boulevard Saint-Laurent Montréal*. But hopes faded when theatrical runs materialized only in Vancouver and Montreal in Canada, and only one or two educational hubs in the northeast US, echoed by the occasional telecast. *Montreal Main*, along with so many treasures of the 1960s and '70s, soon lapsed into almost three decades of legend and obscurity—despite a few precious but wornout VHS cassettes that kept the legend alive in underground and fan circuits—before its 2009 restoration on DVD.

Rubber Gun seemingly confirmed and polished the formula in 1978 with its lingering countercultural pizzazz along with tighter scripting, performances, and narrative, as well as less risk-taking (though still very queer) narrative stakes in sexual politics. *Gun* also had greater success in distribution, but only slightly, and as of 2010 is not available in any format; the rightsholders are seemingly unknown to the director (Moyle 2010). Still, the fertile two decades-long movement had been so diluted by this time that it is possible to see the Moyle-directed film as its swan song—symptomatized by its two Genie nominations, in contrast to *Main*'s terse, seemingly baffled rejection letter from the Academy (always a sign that a Canadian film is doing something right!). Vitale's own retreat from the artisanal mode can also be seen as telling, he lingered as co-cinematographer on his buddy's feature, all the while immersed in the world of exploitation and already reportedly devoted to more industrial undertakings (Massé-Connolly 1978). In Canada it was crystal clear that the CFDC's evolving policies were the smoking gun, most notably the "capital cost allowance" regime initiated in 1977 led to the most arid years in contemporary Canadian cinema. The hybrid, artisanal films produced in early and middle years of the decade had reinvented both narrative-fiction cinema and the documentary and engaged with the baby boomer youth constituency, harnessing a vital creative energy—artisanal and collaborative—that allowed this generation to perceive with new eyes and ears the society around them—and alternative societies—as well as their sexual codes, obsessions, taboos, and utopias. *Montreal Main* recalled in its way earlier cycles of hybrid cinemas that had re-invented realism, such as Italian neo-realism. And whenever successive generations—whether slackers or AIDS activists—would in their turn reinvent a variation, harnessing whatever lighter, cheaper technological breakthrough had suddenly become available, each time the shock of the new and different occasioned by *Montreal Main* would be felt anew. Perhaps that is why this 1974 sleeper still looks so fresh in the era of digital feature gluts and YouTube saturation, still exerts what Peter Brawley, wearing his poet hat, called its "rosy mystery."

THREE: TEXT

The original feature film *Montreal Main* was not officially divided up into episodes, sequences, or "chapters," all the more so since it is constructed in a 1970s-style mosaic of interwoven short vignettes. However, the logic of twenty-first-century DVD production conveniently allows us to divide the flow of the film into sixteen "episodes" in order to best unpack their formal and thematic resonances. In the interests of streamlining, our sixteen "episodes" correspond only roughly to the DVD version's twenty "scenes," and we provide below both the time indications and the duration of each of our episodes based on the DVD.

Episode one: Setup: Two universes (0:0 to 2:20)
The credits unroll over a landscape and zoom in on the slightly decrepit streetscape of Boulevard Saint Laurent in the Plateau Mont-Royal, the storefronts above which Frank and Bozo's low-budget bohemian loft is situated. A domestic argument is heard, and once we enter the loft, we meet the bearded hero Frank, who is simultaneously finishing a transaction with a delivery guy and kicking out his strung-out girlfriend Pam, who clearly has a serious substance habit. An intercut introduces us to another universe, the genteel once-suburban residential neighborhood of Notre-Dame-de-Grâce, where Ann Sutherland is unpacking groceries while gearing

FIGURE 13. The Upper Main, Frank's loft at 4318 Boulevard St-Laurent. DVD still.

up with her husband David for their party. David calls his son Johnny, but the boy doesn't show up.

This opening sets out the title, topic, and setting of the film—the Main, Montreal's Boulevard Saint-Laurent, the traditional immigrants' street of dreams, that divided English from French Montreal.

The upper Main had once been the site of the thriving *shmata* trade, but the sweatshops were gradually emptying and becoming cheap artists' lofts like Frank's. Lower down and closer to the river, the Main also served as the city's red-light district with its decrepit arcade-style pool-room/

FIGURE 14. Homosocial triangle at the Sutherlands: Frank coming between Jackie and Bozo. DVD still.

French-fry joints that constitute a third pole of the film's narrative geography. Five miles (eight km) to the west, on the other side of downtown and past the elite Anglo stronghold of Westmount, is the Sutherland's neighbourhood, Notre-Dame-de-Grâce (NDG), another pole of the film's cinematic space, with its leafy streets and brick houses.[17]

The opening sequence establishes these spatial cores of the film as well as the pattern of intercutting back and forth

17. The area might have been called "Our Lady of Straights," in the 1960s counter-cultural connotation of the term, meaning "conventional" and "uptight" in addition to "heterosexual."

among them, and it also establishes the main characters who inhabit these spaces. Already clear are Frank's heterosexual credentials and the sober moral edge that coexist with his freaky bohemian sensibility and charismatic, dark-bearded look. In the video pre-shoot, the heterosexual credentials were even clearer. The "kick-out-the-girlfriend" scene was more developed and at the same time gentler: there was an erotic post-coital ambience around the couple's farewell, with the languorous, grounded, and together girlfriend played by another of Vitale's real-life exes, future feminist documentarist Anne Henderson. The boy who turns out to be the film's main character has been summoned by his dad but does not appear for another quarter-hour into the film.

Episode two: Two 'families' (2:20 to 6:01)

The downtown and suburban families and worlds are now interwoven as we meet more characters and spaces in a still expository framework: Frank picks up his roommate Bozo on the rainy Main, and they perform a mock-cruising scene in their beat-up Volkswagen van. It's playful and campy but escalates when Frank nearly runs his buddy down and Bozo spits back. Cut to the other universe and a more traditional family, as we see the Sutherlands returning to their house with Bozo's new girlfriend Jackie whom they've just welcomed back "home." The two worlds are interwoven: Bozo consoles Frank over Pam while the two play loft-wall ball, and the Sutherlands talk things over with Jackie.

FIGURE 15. Cruiser and cruisee. DVD still.

Bozo and Frank go to the Sutherlands, where Jackie gives a welcome hug to Bozo while Frank looks on.

The opening continues to emphasize Frank and Bozo's heterosexuality and their availability and thus gives them permission, as filmmakers and characters, to take up this flirtation with queer transgression, to play with boundaries. While the homosocial triangle established along with Bozo and Jackie's reunion threatens to eventually explode, the heterosexual narrative premise gives the artists permission also to take up one of the most controversial subjects of their day and ours, as if under the radar: intergenerational love, or to use its tabloid/scientific term, pedophilia, or the more confrontational label claimed by its political constituency, "man-boy love." Oddly, the cruising scene is the only time we see Frank's playful, campy side, and it is very convincing: otherwise, Frank is a major worrier in a film full of worriers. (Mark Finch called the film "Vitale's worry letter to the 70s" [Finch 1987].) The mock-cruising scene is one of several moments in these expository scenes that are potentially misleading: are we deliberately misled to believe the film might be about Frank and Pam, or about Frank and Bozo getting in deeper rather than torn apart?

It is already clear that this is a great city film, a portrait of Montreal, a place where the bohemia of penniless artists and sexual marginals living in cheap lofts on the Main enter into a tense relationship with the middle-class suburbs. Eric Bloch's fine 16mm color cinematography captures the textures of street space and living space with documentary flare. In this episode, the two worlds come together.

Episode three: The youth clinic (meeting the queer chorus) (6:01 to 8:13)
Frank and Bozo head out in the van to pick up beer, talk more about Jackie, and also about their absent gay friends Steve and Peter, who are not invited to the party. We meet Steve and Peter as they resentfully see Frank and Bozo off to the Sutherlands for the party, while at the other end of town the Sutherlands groom in preparation for their guests and discuss their shy new acquaintance Frank, who is both inconspicuous and conspicuous. Steve and Peter continue to complain about the straight world from which they have just been excluded.

Gay shame enters the picture: however cool Bozo and Frank are, their queeny, kinky, stoned friends are simply not invited to NDG, and however much defiance and indifference Peter and Steve flamboyantly act out, the hurt is felt. Peter and Steve are flaming queer rebels, while Frank and Bozo live more in a liminal world, with one foot in the respectable sphere of McGill University (from which they have just escaped) and this tony West End suburb. (Art meets life: in one set of publicity bios circulating alongside the distribution of the film around 1980, the heterosexual credentials of Vitale, Moyle, and even Lack, all complete with wives and offspring, are foregrounded, and queer ex-con Brawley is not even included.) In any case, in this two-minute interlude, Steve and Peter's key role as queer chorus, commenting on the loves and struggles of their leading-man buddies, is set up—always the astute and bitchy bridesmaids, never the anguished bride.

Episode four: Are you getting a bit hard? (8:13 to 12:38)
On the way to the Sutherlands' party in the van, Frank and Bozo talk through their relationship, each egging the other on to deepen it through sexual experimentation. They stop in a secluded street to try some front-seat mutual masturbation, but dogs start barking, sirens sound, and they feel ridiculous despite "a bit" of tumescence. Along the way, a flash-forward shows a decontextualized Bozo referring to the still unseen Johnny and "the rush of what it must be like to be a homo for an hour" that Frank is about to feel.

So much is going on in this comic scene, as brilliant as it is heavy-handed and implausible. The tandem masturbation is truly weird: Katherine Monk, author of *Weird Sex and Snowshoes and Other Canadian Film Phenomena* (2001) would certainly have approved, had she even been aware of this canonical work amid her skewed corpus. The sequence quite rightly makes Vitale and Moyle cringe to watch it thirty-five years later for the DVD, but it's essential to the film; it breaks the ice. The two pals pretend to be cool: this is "gay chic" way ahead of its time—and, as they say, "all of our friends are gay." But they're also anxious about their conflicted desires and identities, and the dichotomy between too much introspection and not enough ("You always want to gouge out the insides of our relationship," Bozo accuses Frank) sets up a fundamental dynamic for the film, arising later between Bozo and his girlfriend Jackie. This may not be exactly the reductive "essential-existential" dichotomy set up by Peter Harcourt (2002), but he's right—it's a fundamental personality and lifestyle difference that structures the film—and the entire baby boomer generation, for that matter. The Volkswagen jerk-off scene shows the only sex in the film (and you can certainly see very little through the windshield), and significantly it's bad sex, even "ridiculous," as Bozo admits. (This reticence, whether driven by chastity or prudence, no doubt contributed to the almost universal acceptance of the film by critical networks in the mid-1970s. The critical

FIGURE 16. Feeling ridiculous and a bit hard. DVD still.

fraternity took in their stride such comparatively explicit heterosexual works as *Last Tango in Paris* [Bernardo Bertolucci, 1972] and *Don't Look Now* [Nicolas Roeg, 1973], but with some taboos, discretion was the better part of valor.) Frank is clearly more interested than Bozo, though he disavows it, and there's a charm in the clumsiness of needing to ask your partner, whose dick you have in your hand, "Are you getting a bit hard?" But jerk-off moments in public between two twenty-something purportedly straight men, told as Laurel-and-Hardy comedy against a sound backdrop of dogs and cops, are still less risky than the real subject of the film, which has not yet been revealed. The two inspired, discreetly erotic scenes between Frank and Bozo—the mock-cruising scene and the mutual jerk-off scene (both involving the van)—were already clearly in place for the video pre-shoot in the summer of 1972, and were hardly altered when it came to the 16mm shoot several months later.

Episode five: The party (14:19 to 17:53)
Back in suburban NDG, the party guests arrive at the Sutherlands, Bozo and Jackie kiss, and conversations are about careers, while the song "When the Snow Flies" soars on the soundtrack. Alienated Frank, sitting apart on the stairs, is persuaded by Bozo to stay a bit longer. He goes upstairs, snoops around Ann Sutherland's bedroom—in her toiletries and even her letters and purse—and then opens a door to come up behind a long-haired adolescent reading a magazine article about call girls. Frank dons an African mask that's hanging outside the door and sneaks up behind the reader who turns around: it's twelve-year-old Johnny. Their eyes meet, lingering in auspicious close-up.

In this episode, Frank and Bozo explore the scary world of middle-class respectability, chic but suburban and straight. Why is Frank violating Mrs Sutherland's privacy just as he is on the verge of stealing her son? His license as an artist offers us one reason: both Vitale and his character have an ethnographic impulse as a photographer/filmmaker, respectable alibi for the voyeuristic undercurrent of his work, and this impulse is repeatedly and most conspicuously revealed in scenes set in public places.

The big moment of the film arrives: the discovery of

Johnny, who is, significantly, set up as a girl, but—surprise, surprise—it's a beautiful twelve-year-old boy with long hair. In fact, hair is an important motif for the whole movie. Both Johnny's father and his soon-to-be admirer have then-fashionable white Afro dos and facial hair—Frank more so than David—and many of Frank's buddies have unruly, curly shags. In contrast, Jackie wears a prissy, too-neat pixie cut, and Ann has just been seen shaving her legs (and her hairdo seems identical to her son's, something that creates visual echoes a few times in the film). Resonances of testosterone, maturity, and hirsute passion in this predominantly male universe are gravitating—threateningly? lustfully?—around the smooth-skinned pubescent ephebe-hero. To sneak up on his prey, Frank hides behind a black African mask; his Afro fringe, sprouting out from around the ebony edge, evokes a hairy gorilla monster—a tongue-in-cheek pedo stereotype?

Episode six: Two breakfasts, three worlds (17:53 to 21:38)
The Sutherlands breakfast the next morning in their bright kitchen, taking stock of the party, while the tight camera is more interested in Johnny's full, pink lips drinking orange juice. The intercutting shows contrasting worlds: Frank and Bozo talk and drink their coffee in filthy cups filled over a disgusting sink (Frank while sitting on the toilet), as they mock suburbia but still plan to head back to see Jackie and the Sutherlands. Meanwhile, Johnny playfully teases his mother as the bohemians arrive. Frank starts photographing

the family and helps Ann carry in the groceries in a clumsy attempt to obtain permission to take Johnny out on a photography excursion. Johnny hangs out in the garage with his peers, talking about girls, but Frank pops in and removes the impassive boy from the space that belongs to Johnny's generation.

Breakfast in suburbia. The camera delineates the wholesome but chic propriety of the Sutherland family, but the eroticization of Johnny—his sensuality, his lips—steals the show (and has been commented upon by more than one critic).

The bohemian intimacy of the Main is laid out; Frank and Bozo, one of the film's competing couples, share corporeal intimacy and even the joint abjection of bowel habits amid the squalor where they ironically disavow their interest in the straight world. Frank especially avoids acknowledging the impulse he is feeling to pull Johnny into his world. There is much avoidance and dissemblance here and elsewhere in the film, both by characters and by the filmmakers: intradiegetic desire is masked by the artistic alibi of the photographer; extradiegetic authorial desire is masked by the synechdochic close-up aesthetic of the realist 16mm camera. No wonder reviewer Michel Euvrard said the film was full of "unexplored virtualities" (Euvrard 1974).

The breakfast scene was much more developed in the video pre-shoot, including both a nude breakfast-in-bed with Bozo and Jackie's sparring over the latter's dislike of bananas (sometimes, hopefully, a banana is just a banana ...) and an interaction between Johnny and Jackie on the deck. The pruning didn't hurt.

Episode seven: Frank and Johnny on the Mountain (21:38 to 27:16)
Frank and Johnny walk silently up the street to the Mountain—what we locals call Parc Mont-Royal—Frank with his camera in hand and Johnny just sullen enough to imply he might not really be into it. They talk as they walk, but are not miked. Frank takes some photos, and once they are alone in the autumn woods, they relax, lie on the ground, and construct a matchstick palisade that they set alight and then bombard with rocks. When it begins to rain, they retreat to the shelter of the Park's Chalet, where they play "blow the spinning coin around the table," and then head down the other, wilder side of the Mountain, overlooking the city. Frank takes more photos of his model, focusing on his neck and cheek, and then has Johnny stare up into his lens. An abrupt cut shows Frank awakening in his bed with a nightmarish start, as if suddenly aware that something big is happening, and then plodding over in his underwear to look out his window onto the rain-swept Main.

The Mountain is the third pole of reference in the Montreal landscape explored in the film, the historical site of queer underground debauchery (Allen 1998). The Mountain as such is also revealed, as we have seen, in such films as Claude Jutra's *À tout prendre*, and Denys Arcand's *Déclin de l'empire américain*, Lack and Brawley would certainly have shared this subcultural lore with Vitale and Moyle. This scene on the Mountain is one of the most overt moments in the film, but it's also well-disguised by the activities of photography, mentorship, and pyromania. (Pyromania has long been a figure of erotic passion, the surrogate expression of forbidden love—long before Kenneth Anger made *Fireworks* [1947] and John Greyson made *Lilies* [1996].)

Here, the camera and the point of view of the character Frank converge: he is clearly in love, and Johnny—both the character and the actor—is responding to, even flirting with the camera. Frank's nightmare is very interesting, cut in just as the camera has zoomed in tightly on Johnny's face as he looks upward: Frank is clearly aware of the enormity of the path he has entered upon, and there's no turning back … yet. Frank's underwear-clad movement at dawn through his loft, the only time Vitale sets himself up in the film as anything close to beefcake, seems like an irrelevant moody afterthought, without the slightest trace of narcissism. In this sequence, Frank is the queer subject, not the object—particularly when compared to the full-blown eroticism between artist and model, subject, and object in the sylvan posing session we have just watched. It is typical of this dualistic pattern in the dozens of "gay narratives" that I have linked generically to *Montreal Main* that there is no sexual consummation in the literal sense, only the surrogate or metaphorical fucking of playing with fire and photographic capture. In this and the dozens of other such narratives, from Luchino Visconti to Gus Van Sant: "The dualities set up by both photographers and film-makers—mind and body, voice and image, subject and object, self and other, site for identification and site for plea-sure—these dualities remain literally separate. For the most part, narrative denouements, far from celebrating union, posit separation, loss, displacement, sometimes death, and, at the very most, open-endedness." But we are still a full hour from Vitale's very open end. For now, the Mountain scene can be unpacked at greater length: it includes both Frank's childlike regression in the moments of play, flat on his belly, but also contains the mentorial dynamic of the artist-model encounter with all of the aura of sexual empowerment that I have discussed within the heritage of pedagogic eros, and above all the "entirely new narrative mythos" that emerges when the artist's model asserts agency, looks unblinkingly back (Waugh 1993). Johnny does indeed "look back" in this scene, but as he evolves he does much more.

Episode eight: Relationship talk (27:16 to 34:16)
This is an assemblage of conversations in which characters intently discuss their evolving relationships. In the department store at the mall, traveling shots catch Jackie wanting to get serious about their future with Bozo, while Bozo prefers living for the moment and generalized flippancy. Frank, Bozo, Johnny, and Peter pile out of the van and enter Silver's Frites dorées, a major arcade-like fries, video-games, and pool hangout on

the lower Main. Bozo treats Johnny to a hot dog while Frank looks on and then hears out Peter's respectful advice on the perils of his emerging friendship: "You can't crowd a kid." Peter, Bozo, and Johnny play arcade games, and Frank appears an increasingly perturbed onlooker amid the denizens of the neighborhood, photographed in ethnographic mode. There follow two parallel conversations as the group walks up the Main with the traveling camera in pursuit. Peter and a jealous Bozo argue about the "weird and strange" developments between Frank and Johnny, and Frank and Johnny debrief some more. Back at the loft, Frank shows Johnny his voltmeter, and they enjoy the sparks and the intimacy. Unfortunately, this means Johnny is late for supper, and he lies about where he's been. Both David and Jackie are unhappy.

Another loaded series of scenelets of escalating relationship analysis and simmering, and the setpieces—in Frites dorées, on the Main, and in the loft—are the perfect combination of social and spatial observation and leisurely narrative me-ander. Both Johnny and Frank are learning the price they have to pay for their friendship. Although Johnny's loving all the attention he's getting in this idyllic new world, he's also discovering both his own mendacity and his father's chastise-ment. Frank has already lost sleep over how it's unfolding and now his friends are starting to interfere. But what strikes my students most about this delicately observed, location-based dramaturgical progression with all its ethnographic, geographical, and behavioral texture, is the most artificially scripted scene of the film, showcasing the increasingly nasty dynamic between Bozo and Jackie. Jackie Holden was the only professional actor in the film, and her dialogue is clearly among the most scripted, which makes the dynamic between her and Bozo, with their mismatched vocabularies and acting styles, all the more poisonous. This, in turn, set off my students' misogyny alarms and over the course of the subsequent scenes they ring louder and louder. Even reviewers of the day noticed there's not really very much for women in this film—fair enough, since it's a film about guys. But of the females who dare to intrude, Ann and Pam are excellent but are still cameos that are neither very rich nor fine. Jackie is whining and obnoxious, however undeniably she's the undeserving butt of Bozo's callous manipulations. The common thread throughout this seven-minute progression is the formulaic relationship lingo of that decade that was already being branded as narcissistic (Lasch 1978) and so stamps the film with its period flavor. Still it's a wry and evocative touch to set this scene between the heterosexual lovers in Zellers and their next big scene in the mall as well, hinting at the commodity nature of conventional conjugality and its obligations. (In the video pre-shoots, these scenes took place in neutral, non-commercial spaces and had less punch.)

Episode nine: Freedom rides on the Main (34:16 to 39:31)
Nighttime: Steve, Peter, and Bozo enjoy some coke and then cruise the red light section of the lower Main in the

van, commenting on the "chickies" and "basketballs" on the corners. In Notre-Dame-de-Grâce, Johnny steals out of bed and down the stairs in his underwear—his clothes under his arm and his legs luminous in close-up—gets dressed, and hops on his bike. There's a 1970s musical interlude with the throaty song "When the snow flies ... and I am yours," as Johnny pedals the five-mile (eight-km) ride east from suburbia to the Main, his long hair ripples in the breeze, the neon storefronts beckon, and the mobile camera exults in his liberated point of view.

The eroticism of this scene is amazingly frank and exhilarating: I'm not speaking only of the calfcake—though there's no denying that Johnny's underwear scene[18] is more appealing and elaborate than grungy Frank's—it's a film about freedom and escape, or at least about a glimpse of freedom, and the thrilling kinetics of Johnny's escape through the night shapes one of its sublime moments. The snow is not yet flying, but the crisp air of late fall brushing against Johnny's cheeks as he rides down Sainte Catherine Street is almost palpable. (I

18. The scene now looks beyond-the-pale but then seemed well within it. In the next chapter, we discuss the evolving codes of child nudity that *Montreal Main* and its successor films bring to light. Until approximately the year of the *Montreal Main* shoot (1972), nude, same-sex, intergenerational swimming was the norm for the Montreal downtown YMCA, as Johnny and the filmmakers would have known. Only forty years later, in the same institution, thanks to careful policy/policing, nudity is the exception for men or boys, even in the showers and locker room.

Figure 17. Johnny tiptoeing out to escape on his bike. DVD still.

admit that as a cyclist, I place this film right up there at the top of a decade framed at either end by the immortal bicycle films *Butch Cassidy and the Sundance Kid* [George Roy Hill, 1969] and *Breaking Away* [Peter Yates, 1979]). The scene reminds me of another great Canadian youth film and its very similar escape scene: the younger brother in another wonderful Montreal Anglo feature *Don't Let the Angels Fall* (George Kaczender, 1969, and scripted by queer author Timothy Findley). Guy is one year older than Johnny but is also a rebel who runs off in the middle of the night—from Westmount rather than NDG. Guy makes a nocturnal bolt from nuclear family suburbia to climb, much too symbolically, the geodesic dome at Montreal's post-Expo 67 park in the very open-ended last scene of the film. For Guy has no Frank to escape to (Waugh 2006).

Episode ten: Scum (39:31 to 42:04)
Day: In the van again, back on the upper Main, Frank, Bozo, and Jackie pick up two blonde teenybopper hitchhikers, and Bozo acts up and out. He commands the girls to let him put his hand down their fronts, and things escalate until, in a performance of his psycho persona, he screams "You scum!" at the terrorized passengers. His embarrassed friends are no longer having fun: "Jesus Bozo, cut it out," Jackie tells him.

Immediately counterbalancing Johnny's escape are two other young adolescents on the lam, girls this time, and as their bad luck would have it, they run into Bozo. A cautionary tale for restless kids, a barb at patriarchal culture, or just the next phase in Bozo's deliberate demolition of his relationship with Jackie? This very strange scene may be what clinched the bad taste in the mouths of my feminist students, but it's even scarier in the video pre-shoot, where Bozo grabs the T-shirt of one of the girls, and his companions don't intervene. No wonder the twenty-first century Moyle finds this scene too embarrassing to watch.

Episode eleven: The Main and the mall (42:04 to 46:46) [
Johnny and his pal Tony go back to Frites dorées on the lower Main. A drag queen primps in the photo booth, and the boys play the prize-claw machine when they are cruised by a smiling fiftysomething trench-coater. Steve suddenly shows up, coming to the rescue, chases off the older man, and

FIGURE 18. Bozo acts up. DVD still.

delivers a rapid-shot motormouth rap about the dangers of the "the tiled urinal of Bablyon": "You boys are lucky I got rid of that asshole, the guy was ready to leech on you." The boys are dumbstruck and take off. Steve continues his rap while walking beside the shop windows in the Alexis Nihon Plaza, a few miles to the west on the border of the anglophone suburbs of Westmount and NDG. He visits Peter, who works an ice-cream stall, and finds him with Bozo and Jackie. Jackie is not impressed by what the fags' passive-aggressive innuendos are insinuating about her boyfriend's sexuality and storms off. Bozo catches up with her on the mall escalator and tries to mollify her, explaining that they're just trying to get to know her—to no avail.

Frank isn't in this episode, which is significant since this is where Johnny and his friend are rescued from a stereotypical "child molester," with his oily smile and trench coat. Whether or not this is the intent, the effect is to inoculate the narrative, to disavow what the film is really about. The video pre-shoot's four-way rap session on Frank and Johnny elaborated in detail on the *Death in Venice*/chickenhawk fate that Peter, Bozo, and Steve flippantly claimed to want to save him from: "Thirty years from now, I don't want to see Frank on the streets with a facelift, white vinyl shoes, a little rouge here, lips going like crazy." The film version limits the pedophilic specter to this one glimpse of a suitably Brylcreemed extra recruited on the spot, but in any case, Steve's wild "rescue" is probably more traumatic to the kids than any trench coat encounter might have been.

The glitzy upscale mall is another matter: here, real relationship terror is enacted, though Steve and Peter may have been right to try to rescue their pal Bozo from Jackie, and Jackie may have been prudent to extract herself from an open-bi relationship. Bozo's effort to calm Jackie down is the latest bout of unsuccessful relationship talks between Frank and Pam, Frank and Johnny, Frank and Bozo, and Bozo and Jackie, with continuous commentary from the chorus of un-attached queers.

Episode twelve: Sparks (46:46 to 59:32)
The loft: Frank and Johnny are playing with electrical gadgets again, but Frank appears deep in thought. They look at the spread of Frank's photographs of family and friends

on the walls, and Frank asks Johnny the "big question,"
i.e., what he thinks about their relationship, "You know,
why we're friends, why we like people like you." We get
a glimpse of the Sutherlands still worrying, and then back
at the loft Steve bursts in and finds Johnny hanging out,
realizing that the kid he encountered at Frites dorées is
Frank's new "friend" that he's heard about. Steve tries
to bring him out and still thinks coming on hard with a
motormouth rap is the way to do it. Back in NDG, Ann
Sutherland also tries to get Johnny to open up, asking him
what Frank and he do when they're together. Johnny's terse
reply is, "We just fool around." On the Main, Johnny and his
four adult friends put on genderfuck makeup in preparation
for a night on the town; the kid responds ambiguously to
the campfest, and Peter declares himself "the only one
who's obviously a queen around here." Frank and Bozo
remove their makeup and argue about Johnny. Steve and
Bozo then browse through the former's tabloid newspaper
collection, and the lurid narratives of child murder and
sexual excess make them think of Frank and Johnny. At the
Sutherlands, David is still worried and so is Jackie, who
then joins Bozo on a rooftop for a good knockdown breakup:
she repeatedly calls him a manipulative and "supercilious"
"son of a bitch," to which Bozo ripostes that she's "just like
the Sutherlands: hip on the outside, scared and nervous
about things on the inside." At the loft, Frank's on the
phone hunting for Johnny, and Pam is suddenly back, still
strung out and chewing up the scenery.

The film's central romantic relationship plot is never consummated. When Frank finally inaugurates his own relationship talk with his inamorato in this scene, Johnny either doesn't know anything about sex or just likes the attention, caring, and respect of his much-older friends, so he gives what may be seen as a flirtatious or coy smile of assent. In any case, he feels comfortable. Everyone's trying to get Johnny to talk more; Frank's a bit more successful than either Steve or Ann. There is also some subtle gender play going on in the characterization of these figures: mother and son resemble each other, and Pam, who can't stay away from Frank, is boyish. As for the film's traditionally gendered couple, Jackie and Bozo, nothing became their romance like its ending. Bozo's really talking about himself—as well as the movie, the country, and the entire decade—in his line about hip on the outside but scared on the inside, and almost every reviewer quoted it. In the video pre-shoot, Jackie contributes emphatically to the escalation of the Sutherlands' trepidation about their son and Frank. She doesn't know how to respond when David asks her if her friends Frank and Bozo are queer, and her badgering of Bozo about what's going on with the intergenerational pair contributes directly to the breakup. The film version eliminated this dynamic and was content to maintain a suggestive and ambiguous parallel between the hetero and homo couples.

Figure 19. Steve haranguing Frank's "new friend." DVD still.

Episode thirteen: Outing (59:32 to 1:06:27)

In a convenience store near the Main, Steve and Bozo can't stop talking about their friend ("Frank is fucked"), but a comic storekeeper with a rubber face keeps announcing his wares to relieve the stress. Back in his own apartment above the Jewish gravestone merchant, Bozo answers the phone and agrees to meet Frank out on the street in five minutes for their excursion to Lachute. But out on the street, Frank runs into Johnny, who's playing hooky and takes over Bozo's seat in the van, which doesn't go over very well with Bozo when he joins them. A spirited Jew's harp score accompanies this outing to the livestock fair northwest of the Island of Montreal, but once there the tension rises again. Bozo suggests to Johnny that they try to lose Frank in the crowd, and he makes sarcastic jokes about Frank as they watch a "fine gelding" being auctioned off (Johnny is oblivious to the humor). Frank is left to wander around looking frustrated amid the rich ethnographic canvas. Yet another geezer in the film's portrait gallery of elderly characters puts in a cameo as a passenger in the van on the way home, teaching Bozo a Québécois folksong. Frank drives through the night with the sleeping boy's head resting peacefully in his lap.

Other than Peter-as-ice-cream-vendor's "Bonjour!" cap, this bilingual auction and country fair, followed by the folksong, are almost the only reflections of Quebec's French environment and the only glimpse of the metropolis's hinterland in the film. The sequence resonates with Vitale's characteristic people-watching panache. Frank—with his worried look, recycled black-and-yellow YMHA menorah jersey, and camera slung over his shoulder—looks every inch a sexy American McGill grad discovering Quebec for the first time. Bozo's monopolization of Johnny is amped up now that Jackie's been sent packing, and includes some rambunctious roughhouse. The crescendo toward rupture and even violence continues. But why does Johnny accede? Is he "less attached to Frank than we thought" (Greyson 2009), or is he oblivious to the mindfuck games going on between his two adult friends, or simply a suggestible, passive go-with-the-flow kind of kid when he's feeling comfortable? The blocking of the sequence of the van interior, with Johnny's sleeping face on Frank's thigh, is beatific, wonderfully over-the-top.

FIGURE 20. Bozo and Johnny at the livestock auction. DVD still.

Episode fourteen: Explosions (1:06:27 to 1:15:00)
Upon returning home that night, Johnny finds his parents
are out, and he can't get into the house, so he heads over to
Tony's. Frank and Bozo end up at Schwartz's smoked meat
joint on the upper Main, both very tense. The Sutherlands
come home and can't find their son; the phone rings in
Frank's empty loft. Johnny and Tony lie in bed debriefing
about the day, shirtless under the quilt, when David arrives
to apologetically take his son home. Bozo confronts Frank
about "game playing" and taunts him aggressively, while the
intercutting to the Sutherlands becomes increasingly tighter.
David forbids his son further contact with Frank, and Johnny
talks back to his father, increasingly angry, accusing him
of "prejudice," and finally calling him a "stupid pig" before
David strikes him on the face.

At Schwartz's, when Bozo declares feelings that he says Frank is too obtuse to read and goads him physically, Frank turns the deli table over on his friend. A regular bar room brawl is barely averted by the Schwartz's customers; Bozo screams at Frank: "Pay your bill, you moron!" echoing Johnny's outburst with David. The next morning in the mall, Johnny and Tony argue about whether they should go over to the now verboten Main, and Frank gets a call from David to come down to his office. The David-Frank confrontation is interpolated by a decontextualized cut-away to another lecture from Steve, who warns Frank against pinning the kid to the wall like a butterfly. He makes things explicit: "You fell in love with him," and tells him not to "vampiriz[e] this kid." David meets Frank—specially suit-coated for the purpose—in his tony office, and orders him not to see his son; he asks Frank to agree to a "complete cutoff." Frank doesn't know how to respond except to ask, "I'm a human being, aren't I?" On the way home on the metro, he watches a heterosexual couple publicly kissing before turning his gaze into the dark underground tunnel.

The extended intercut sequences in this episode form the two climactic confrontations of the film's plot, one between Frank and Bozo and the other within the triangle of Frank, Johnny, and paternal castrator David—plus the queer chorus's commentary. *Montreal Main*'s dramatic arc can almost be called conventional, given that these explosions are timed to start like clockwork twenty minutes

FIGURE 21. Cinematographer Eric Bloch videotaping David and Johnny in their "explosion" scene, summer 1972. Production still.

from the film's end. Shy, inarticulate Johnny is seen to be verbally articulate for the first time in film, correctly fobbing the relatively sophisticated concept of "prejudice" at his uptight father before he screams the very counterculture term of abuse, "pig." No wonder ex-hippie David goes berserk and assaults his son. If only Frank, a visual artist, could also be articulate, for "I'm a human being, aren't I?" is a poor defense. The all-too-articulate Steve traumatizes Frank with unasked-for moralism about vampirization, but it helps the film lay its cards on the table to have someone use the word "love." This and the earlier decontextualized flash commentary (Bozo's cynical dig about Frank's "homo rush" in episode four) must have come out of a heavy editing session, where some strong material was heading for the floor but the need for more analytic pointers was still being felt. It's the two out gay men, Steve and Peter, who warn Frank, the closet case, to respect Johnny's independence and integrity. I don't think they do this out of pedophobia, for they respect the principle of Frank's attraction and address Johnny's autonomy rather than the surrounding social panics as the moral issue at stake.

The brawl is another great scene in a Montreal landmark, Schwartz's Hebrew Delicatessen, on the upper Main on the edge of the Plateau Mont-Royal. This neighborhood is now gentrified and has the most expensive real estate in the core area, with huge lineups of tourists and suburban refugees outside of Schwartz's—now called Charcuterie hébraique. I don't know for sure what this mystique around the recognition of familiar community space, so important to "minor cinemas" like Canadian and queer cinema, means to viewers who don't share it. (The same year as the *Montreal Main* shoot, Ted Kotcheff's *The Apprenticeship of Duddy Kravitz* did a location shoot in another Plateau monument of Jewish culture, the Bain Colonial, a vintage bathhouse two blocks away, and the effect is equally magical for us Plateau dwellers.) In such scenes, there are cues, which I suspect the insiders don't notice, that this space is holy ground. Perhaps something as mundane as the loving documentary attention devoted to the slicing of brisket, or the unquestionable authenticity of the extras.

Episode fifteen: Johnny takes action (1:15:00 to 1:23:06)
David pounds on Johnny's bedroom door, but the boy has
locked himself in. Pam has returned to Frank's, and rails,
not unreasonably, against the clutter in his loft: "This is a
dungeon." Johnny has a clash with Ann and won't answer
her question, "What's the matter with you lately?" He runs
out of the house, slamming the door, then takes a bus across
town to the Main, where he pokes his head in the door at
Frank's. Their conversation is to the point:

"You're amazing ..."

"I want to stay here ..."

"I can't be your new father ..."

"But we were friends ..."

"I didn't ... You can't stay here ..."

"Are you afraid of my father?"

"I'm afraid of him ... Okay, so fucking what?"

Frank resourcefully takes Johnny for a walk through the
decrepit back streets of the Plateau, and then sends them into
a corner store to buy them Cokes. Johnny emerges from the
store to find that Frank has disappeared. Johnny runs, as if
for his life, down the streets, and soon drops the bottles. After
a few blocks, he comes to rest, leaning despondently against

a wall, while kids play in the alley behind him. The sequence ends in close-up profile on Johnny's face.

This is the devastating dénouement of the film: Johnny takes his life into his hands, asserting full agency without realizing that society doesn't allow twelve-year-olds to do so, and the scene ends in utter betrayal, cowardice, and abandonment. Frank's bad faith is encapsulated in his pretense that this is about his being Johnny's surrogate father. In the historical context, few other endings for the film (or the relationship) could have been possible. At least it's not what we might then have reductively called a "dead queer" movie such as *Death in Venice* or *Dreamspeaker*. As John Greyson says, "The very inconclusiveness of the gentle ending is a telling transgression of gay '70s cinematic narrative traditions ... the sort of story-telling that we all need to be reminded of: questioning, nuanced, unresolved and deeply human, one where all three sides of this triangle are allowed to walk away, and to wonder" (2009). For better or worse, Frank's abandonment of Johnny may well have been the precondition for the critical acclaim that greeted the film.

Episode sixteen: Dénouement (1:22:05 to 1:27:46)
David bursts in on Frank, virtually assaulting him: "Where is he?" Frank is apologetic, saying "I didn't mean to fuck everything up." Later, Bozo serves Frank coffee in the traditional filthy mugs as they take stock. Frank is again apologetic, wondering about his unconscious motives to screw

FIGURE 22. After breakups and bust-ups, Frank and Bozo's happy ending
... in the movie only. DVD still.

up Bozo and Jackie or the Sutherlands. The scene ends with
a comradely conciliatory cuddle, Bozo kneading his friend's
tense back. But things remain up in the air: "I feel sort of like
... I don't know," mumbles Frank. The coda returns to familiar
images of the solitary denizens of Frites dorées, the electric
game machines pinging and pool table clacking, and as the
camera comes in close, Johnny is gradually revealed, rifle
on his shoulder, intently playing the shooting game, again in
extremely tight profile. The concluding shot is the now-storied
Frites dorées façade; the credits roll, and the song "Brother,
who do you think you are?" comes up.

Frank continues on his path of cowardice and retraction. At
least his final line, "I don't know," may hint at some possible
level of self-awareness. In the video pre-shoot of this scene,

FIGURE 23. Johnny gets his gun ... and his movie. DVD still.

Frank intones, "I don't know if I was trying to fuck up you and Jackie, to fuck up the Sutherlands ... to fuck Johnny ..." But in the final celluloid version, this line is tellingly different, omitting the last option and lowering the ante considerably.

The apparent recuperation of Frank and Bozo's relationship suggests a happy ending, and a likely reading is the affirmation of Frank and Bozo's erotic-tinged bromance. But this *faux* ending is the surface resort of the scriptwriter and only that: surely no thinking spectator can imagine that Bozo has got back what he's wanted all along—Frank—and that everything will return to normal with the survival of their homosocial friendship.

And what about the "Johnny Gets His Gun" parting shot? A newly empowered but equally embittered Johnny, alone

FIGURE 24. Ethnographic trope of lower Main "decrepitude." DVD still.

for the second time in the film—with a new awareness of the perfidy of adults and the world—gets ready for the sequel that never came. Endings are important. Frank has dithered away offscreen, and—visually, dramatically, and politically—the movie has become Johnny's movie.

Back to the Main, and this fine city film ends where it began. Well, not quite; the decrepit lower Main is different from the upper Main that launched the film. In the spring of 2010, as this book was being written, the French-fry/billiard arcades were all boarded up and slated for demolition, and the famous drag club Cléopâtre, immortalized by *Il etait une fois dans l'Est*, was clinging to life in the face of plans to develop a glitzy entertainment district—as were the hookers, for both place and people were equally threatened by the gentrifiers' and developers' wrecking ball.

FOUR: SEXTEXT: Intergenerational Cinema and Politics

Queer camp, according to Jon Davies in his book on Paul Morrissey's *Trash*, is almost Christ-like in its loving promiscuity, shining its light on the whole of discarded humanity, as evidenced by the film's trans-protagonist Holly's reclamation of the trashed people and things she finds in the streets. Davies claims, quoting Robert Stam at length, that "the ethos of queer camp ... at its heart [is] the bestowing of value and love on to that which has been neglected or reviled. [... G]arbage is a 'truth teller' that 'signals the return of the repressed:' it is the 'ultimate resting place of all that society produces and represses, secretes and makes secret.'" This human refuse "include[s] all those people left over from mainstream society," carrying with them the promise "'that anyone can be redeemed, no matter how lowly and degraded ... a reminder that we are all in some way the same, of equal potential and equal value, and there is a precious quality discoverable in all us meager products'" (Stam, in Davies 2009, 15–16, 135, 163).

This illustrates the quasi-religious framework of sexual identity politics and gestures to the painful false promise of its purported universalism when it comes to its own truth-telling garbage. Now that the gay and lesbian movement is almost fully mainstreamed, we might stop to ask upon whom the glory of camp fails to shine its redemptive light.

The queer community represented by Vitale, Moyle, Lack, and Brawley is long gone. So too are its real-world political and cultural counterparts, like the Boston radical tabloid *Fag Rag*, some of whose contributors have gone silent or underground. The openness and sensitivity to nuance and difference that marked the era, the basic respect and curiosity required to do justice to Frank and Johnny's relationship, have since been obliterated in the West. We recover *Montreal Main* as an error of the nascent LGBTQ movement, a genomic sequence too mutagenic for the clique that runs GLAAD (Gay & Lesbian Alliance Against Defamation), a palette of possibilities too far ranging for a community held secure behind the rainbow gates of "between consenting adults."

This chapter attempts to recover the aesthetics and politics of what most people think of as a bygone issue, a task some readers may find challenging or even outrageous. If we disagree on many things, let us agree on one thing: that nothing in our society is as silenced as Frank and Johnny's relationship. Now let it speak, let it challenge, let it outrage a little, as we explore *Montreal Main*'s cinematic and political intertexts, which help us understand why the film remains such a surprise today.

Is Montreal Main *a queer film?*

Frank and Johnny's friendship does not arrive unannounced, even if it appeared, at the time, to emerge out of nowhere. Today's audience multiplies the relationship's seriousness by what has been registered culturally over the past forty years, the abuse narrative. Frank is not just a man interested in boys, but a potential molester or "pedophile" whom we have the right to fear. Johnny is not just a boy interested in a man, but a potential "victim" for whom we have the right to fear. A product of accident and improvisation, *Montreal Main* has gotten better with age, as the genre of intergenerational sexuality has taken on the qualities of a noir thriller—all shadows, suspense, and bloody murder. The audience has been placed at the edge of their seats.

The stock character of the child abuser has a cinematic history that extends well beyond its present-day therapeutic institutionalization. An early image comes from the film *M* (Fritz Lang, 1931), starring Peter Lorre as Hans Beckert, a serial-killing child molester hunted by not only the police but also the entire criminal underworld. When Beckert is finally caught, he wails, "I can't help myself! I have no control over this, this evil thing inside of me, the fire, the voices, the torment!" In Claude Jutra's *Le Dément du lac Jean-Jeunes* (*The Madman of Jean-Jeunes Lake*, 1948), an eleven- or twelve-year-old boy is sequestered by his "demented" father, a crazed hermit living in a cabin, until the Boy Scouts arrive to retrieve their friend, pushing the monster off a cliff

FIGURE 25. *M*: "I can't help it!" DVD still. © Nero-Film AG

and to his death (Waugh 2006). He is not literally a sexual abuser, but sexuality is in the air of this wonderfully incoherent melodrama, whose Scout rescuers are blatantly eroticized by Jutra's lens. The man is ugly, imbecilic, gangly, and awkward, dirty from his crooked hat down to the toes poking out through his shoes. He brutalizes his son, forcing him to do his bidding. Although today we reject these characterizations as exaggerations, since we know abusers are mostly everyday people, our need to continually remind ourselves of this ordinariness tells us how compelling the generic characterization continues to be.

Frank's bohemian normality masks, narratively, his "true" nature as a sex offender (though some viewers will derive a thrill from contemplating whether he is or whether he isn't). The main question asked of the film used to be, "Is he gay or isn't he?" "The film might be characterized as a 'homosexual' rather than 'gay' film, since it never carries its theme to its logical conclusion ... Latent homosexuality is rampant, particularly in the highly erotic relationship between Frank and Johnny, which the characters themselves do not perceive as homosexual in nature" (Dayman 1974). Today, the audience gets to play US Red Scare Senator Joseph McCarthy by interrogating Frank, "Are you now, or have you ever been, a member of the pedophile party?" By avoiding sexual consummation, the film maintains its fundamental inscrutability, and Frank returns to the shadows as dangerous as ever, a threat perceived but not proven, one to watch until the fateful day when—perhaps he doesn't see us watching—he commits his crime. At that moment, the whole weight of the ritual of public humiliation can be enacted by the usual suspects (the police, the media, and the vigilantes), while the queer community stands by and watches or perhaps even applauds. Frank becomes even more threatening by failing to prove his guilt, failing to draw himself within the lines of the cartoonish "pedophile."

It's difficult to imagine a time when this kind of suspicion was not a universal interpretive norm, when Frank could still just be Frank, a fumbling, bumbling desirer of he-knows-not-what. The heritage of stereotype and stigma found in *M* and *Le Dément* was rejected in the wake of post-Stonewall gay pride by organizations like the Paedophile Information Exchange (PIE), formed in 1974, and the North American Man/Boy Love Association (NAMBLA), founded in 1978. At that time, the sexual, gay, lesbian, and child liberation movements paved the way for a rethink. Boy-love activists believed in the power of coming out, being represented and heard, and participating openly in the mobilizations of allied political movements. The cringing of *M*'s Hans Beckert was replaced by a language of pride in one's desire, as men (and some women) came out as boy lovers, making the shocking suggestion that they were people who wanted to love and do no harm.

The radical boy-love cinema of 1970s French avant-garde director Lionel Soukaz (Youmans 2009; Dyer 1990) marked a high watermark of radical erotic rethinking of pedophile desire; Soukaz's films mixed 8mm footage of pubescent boys loitering and lounging in parks and beside public fountains with erotic and sometimes explicitly pornographic imagery obtained from publicly available skin mags like *Piccolo* and *David*, whose cover-boy, "Lukas," maintains a following to this day. Not only was the formerly shameful declared a point of pride, but the unseen became seen, the unknown knowable—for those who wanted to look. The smiling, willing, and aroused participation of the boys stamped the emerging politics with an easy legitimacy: men and boys enjoyed each other. This politics and these images, combined with the momentum of other liberation movements, seemed to shake the old stereotypes to their foundations, and some sensed great changes in the air.

However, at the same time, the old narrative underwent a revolution of its own and was updated and made militant. The idea of child abuse, which had not yet been dominated by the concept of sexual abuse, as illustrated in *Le Dément*, was finally merged with feminist anti-rape activism by the mid-'70s. Through grassroots consciousness-raising and the therapeutic confessional, a culture of "coming out" to experiences of rape and sexual trauma appeared, producing identity for women as survivors of a psychotically patriarchal system. Rape was seen to be not merely a personal assault but a tool of male-dominated society at its worst when subjecting children to its power.

Johnny Sutherland, therefore, cuts the perfect figure of a victim: barely pubescent, small, shy, and submissive, unaware of the complexities of the adult world, unaware of Frank's desire. In this version of events, Frank is a schemer, plotting to get into the pants of poor Johnny, who is easily fooled, just a kid—so inexperienced, knowing nothing, desiring nothing—just a target for the action of others who do not necessarily have his best interests at heart. Johnny cannot detect what is going on, and even if he could, he wouldn't be able to articulate it. According to this view, as Frank rubs the raw nerve of his sexuality on Johnny's face, the boy can only lie there passively, taking in and never giving, until years later, when the traumatic memories begin flooding back.

The child liberationist ethos, which began with declarations by proto-pedophile pediatrician Janusz Korczak in the 1920s, had become politically radical in the 1960s and '70s. Radical critiques of education (Holt 1974; Goodman 1956; Illich 1970) suggested turning young people loose and allowing them to exercise a will of their own. But the right to be free quickly transformed, in legal and cultural practices, to a right to be protected, a right to be educated, a right, essentially, to the paternalistic control of the state and family. In this transitional moment, questioning was possible, but a "person"—defined as a child well beyond tender years—was becoming a target of "benign" control, a subject who can will the proper things only through the prism of state and parental control. Their will to sexuality for all intents and purposes denied, the Johnnys of the world can only be targets of aggressive maniacs. The child liberation movement was not tempered by wise observation, but transformed into its opposite, something that gave no respect to the individual case. The boys of *David* and *Piccolo* were (and continue to be) deemed aberrations, errors created by "pedophiles," rather than seen as individuals with histories and meanings of their own who could be admitted as additional truths of our culture.

Gay male politics were not as firmly linked to an analysis

of rape. Boyd McDonald's legendary *Straight to Hell* news-letter accepted, beginning in 1973, first-person accounts of experiences of violence and sexual extremes as legitimate narratives of male sexuality. Many lesbians, informed by the growing feminist movement, were very early critics of man-boy love, one New York City group "Lesbians Arising" writ-ing in 1980, "The ultimate resolution of this issue would be the legalization of the rape of young boys who are in the traditional position of women in this society" (in Tsang 1981, 125). One sign of this difference of opinion within the community was the division, into two separate marches, of the 1980 New York City Pride march because some lesbians refused to march with NAMBLA.

This internal critique was also given the vast support of the politicized morality of the Silent Majority, championed by evangelical Christians like Anita Bryant. Finding com-mon cause in a critique of sex and pornography, the Right and conservative feminism brought pressure from both in-side and outside the movement to fracture boy-love politics, pushing it to the sidelines and muting its supporters. Child pornography (which has always also meant adolescent por-nography) was the weapon used against the gay movement, along with the "homosexuals-are-child-molesters" political cliché. This was half true. As we have seen in Chapter One, gay organizations had a history of critiquing the age-of-con-sent legalism. NAMBLA really was an early member of good standing in the International Gay and Lesbian Association

(IGLA). Boy-lovers really did help produce seminal papers like *Fag Rag*.

These activities and organizations were vulnerable to the slander. Immense internal and external pressures, including criminal prosecution, hollowed out organizations like PIE and NAMBLA, causing them to buckle and fall into various scandals, culminating, for example, in the destruction of substantial parts of the scholarly Brongersma archive by Dutch police.[19] For a brief period, the West was at a crossroads: would it view intergenerational sexuality as something involving people or monsters? The West chose monsters.

Child abuse, a concept under development during the 1970s, became hardened around a new center: child *sexual* abuse. A new understanding was developed on the therapist's couch that stressed the role of trauma-induced amnesia, memory recovery, and interpretive reworking of experience. And it was accompanied by a narrative of sexual assault that stressed threats, force, violation, and disturbance as the characteristics of adults erotically interested in minors. I call this the "abuse narrative" and it provided an answer to the questions people had about why these events occur and what to do about it. Articulating and making permanent certain categories (of perpetrator, victim, adult, child, abuse, etc.)

---

19. For an account of this document collection by the Dutch jurist and scholar Edward Brongersma (1907–1994) and its liquidation, see *www.ipce.info/ipceweb/Library/guide_brong_01feb_eng.htm*, and *www. iisg.nl/exhibitions/censorship/brongersma1.php*.

granted power over the complicated and often confusing matter of intergenerational sexuality. It has been a story repeated endlessly in media portrayals, related by therapists to their clients, filling a hundred books as well as the coffers of the "abuse industry" (Waugh 2011). It is the "way things are" about intergenerational sexuality in our time.

Even though the abuse narrative has played out in incredible excesses—in false memory therapy, the McMartin (1983–90) and other daycare scandals, the Satanic ritual abuse conspiracy theory, to name just a few—it has not only secured itself a place in the public mind, but made impossible the circulation of any alternative. The overwhelming social pressure, silencing of critics, and evaporation of funds for alternate research has resulted in anemic and one-sided knowledge: "The systematic exploration of the subjective experience of minors involved in sexual contact with adults ... has generally been absent in the literature" (Clancy 2009, 57). Editor Ken Plummer reported that there were zero articles on pedophilia and only one on child sexuality submitted in ten years to the cutting-edge British journal *Sexualities* (2008). A handful of articles have appeared on the subject in the queer journal *GLQ*, often one-off's about film (Ohi 2000; Angelides 2004; Davies 2007). In contrast, the well-established academic institutions that regularly produce books and articles on the subject are funded by government agencies to aid law enforcement. One such institution, COPINE, spells it out quite clearly: Combating Paedophile Information Networks in Europe: an attack not only on child pornography, but on the very idea of "pedophile"—read boy-love—activism. Nothing outside of the condemnatory framework, which grows in power every day, is allowed.

Defenders of the hegemonic abuse narrative argue that any belief that would encourage sexual activity between adults and minors is a delusion. In 2007, a Scout Leader in Australia, for example, was sent to prison for ten years; it was reported that the fact the man regarded his victims as his friends and said they consented to sexual activity had shown his disturbing lack of insight (Fewster 2009). That "delusion" is the main counterpoint, that any other opinion could not be grounded in fact, says a lot about how the child sexual abuse narrative has succeeded in monopolizing reality. And the delusional, of course, must be sent to re-education camps such as Coalinga.[20]

Under pressure from right-wing politicians in the United States, the International Lesbian and Gay Association

---

20. Coalinga is a psychiatric prison in California where men who have served their time in prison for sex crimes are civilly committed without hope of release because of the essentially fictional exit policies. The only film about the Coalinga detainment facility is the BBC TV documentary *Louis Theroux: A Place for Paedophiles* (2009), a hand-wringing piece more concerned with the eponymous filmmaker's attempt to judge the "pedophiles" he meets and to participate in the functions of psychiatric justice than to conduct a serious evaluation.

in 1994 expelled all organizations that were said to defend
"pedophiles."[21] This was a watershed moment that stamped
the gay and lesbian seal of approval on a new de facto policy
of exclusion of boy love within the LGBTQ community. In
the same year, the Gay & Lesbian Alliance Against Defamation, an organization that helps keep the image of gay and
lesbian identity neat and tidy, declared NAMBLA to be outside the LGBTQ fold, defining its politics as child abuse.[22]
It is not unfair to say that the LGBTQ community has, since
then, in part defined itself as being not about child and intergenerational sexuality. They have left the Franks of the
world to be "disappeared" by monstrous institutions like the
sex offender registries and civil commitment prisons; they
have left Frank to be thrown out with the trash.

And it isn't that different in the radical corners of queer
theory, notwithstanding the boasts of Eve Kosofsky Sedgwick, who claimed queer was an "open mesh of possibilities, gaps, overlaps, dissonances and resonances, lapses and
excesses of meaning [wherein] the constituent elements of
anyone's gender, of anyone's sexuality aren't made (or can't
be made) to signify monolithically" (*Tendencies* 1995, 8).

---

21. See Wikipedia article, "International Lesbian, Gay, Bisexual,
Trans and Intersex Association."

22. See "GLAAD/USA Position Statement Regarding NAMBLA,"
*www.qrd.org/qrd/orgs/GLAAD/general.information/1994/position.
on.nambla-02.22.94*

Somehow, for all that, Sedgwick forgot at least one telling category from her famous list of "flaming," "shame-cre-ative," and "performative identity vernaculars:" including "... butch abjection, femmitude, leather, pride, sm, drag, musicality, fisting, attitude, zines, histrionicism, asceticism, Snap! Culture, diva worship, florid religiosity ..." (Sedgwick 1993a, 13–14). Queers have been more than capable of sig-nifying intergenerational sexuality as "not welcome."

Queer theory began in great part with David Halperin's 1989 essay "One Hundred Years of Homosexuality," which he claims was born out of a desire to avoid applying con-temporary conceptual frameworks to ancient history and to return Greek pederasty to its "indigenous meanings" (Halperin 2002, 4). Yet Halperin relied on a feminist power-analysis of rape, vintage 1989, neglecting the subtleties of Foucault, focusing blindly on strict binaries of homosexual-ity and heterosexuality, active and passive, all without ad-dressing relevant differences between the experiences of free-born boys and house-bound Athenian women. Having pressed the right political buttons, Halperin provided the then institutionalizing gay and lesbian studies movements a wholesome excuse for neglecting intergenerational sexuality. As one critic put it: "Halperin's strongly negative portrayal of Greek pederasty coincided with the systematic strategy of mainline, assimilationist gay rights organizations to mar-ginalize any consideration of youth sexuality or reform in age-of-consent laws and instead present to the public the most unthreatening, plain vanilla image of gays and lesbians (Hubbard 2000, 6)."

ILGA purged NAMBLA in 1994 at the peak of the queer theory surge in academia, yet queer theorists have published almost nothing—either then or thereafter—about this fraught moment or its political and social effects, nor on any of the institutions of control that have ballooned since that time. Although Lee Edelman is the author of *No Future*, which "argues that the child is the 'perpetual horizon' of every politics" (Davies 2007, 378; Edelman 2004), he nevertheless refuses to address the political realities generated by "reproductive futurism" as they apply to the ontological other of the child—the pedophile. Instead, in a clownish theoretical contrivance, Edelman linked Pascal's theory of 1 and 0 to anal rape of children in Pedro Almodovar's *La mala educación* (*Bad Education*, 2004) since, obviously, 1 looks like a penis, and 0 looks like an anus (Edelman 2008). No matter how effusive the queer theorists can be about the blurry boundaries of queer, "everyone knows" it does not include man-boy love.

Mainstream gay and lesbian politics have entirely overlooked the institutional effects of the pedophile panic. Feminist scholar and activist Erica Meiners points out that "LGBT organizations have been silent" about sex offender registries, even though queers have been "historically defined as sex offenders" (Meiners 2009, 4). This statement not only underlines the complicit silence of LGBTQ political communities, but also reveals how political queers have defined the Franks of the world out of "queer." If Frank is queer, then queers are not *historically* defined as sex offenders, but are so at the present time. If, on the other hand, Frank is not queer, the sex-offender issue is historical for the queer community. The sex offender registries, the institutions of civil commitment, and the increasing surveillance of the state can be assessed as politically relevant for the LGBTQ community only insofar as these institutions "could potentially augment 'fear of the queer'" (ibid.). Instead of dealing in the realities of the lived experience of those targeted by the institutions, political queers focus on the "potentiality" of relevance to communities that are not directly targeted. Thus, even radical queer activism neutralizes the boy lover (now pedophile, now sex offender) so that he has no subjectivity worth defending. A historical meeting, bringing "sex offenders" and queer academics together for the first time, "What's Queer About Sex Offenders?" Conference at the Gay Community Center in Chicago, took place in 2010, a full nineteen years after Minnesota's 1991 sex offender registry legislation. One professor in attendance declared, "It's too late" to do anything about the sex offender system, even if we wanted to. No LGBTQ group criticized the bill proposing the death penalty for pedophiles that would have made child pornography an executable offense in Texas (Hughes 2007; Andriette 2007). Years of queer inaction have produced the conditions of political passivity in the post-exclusion era.

The relevance of this discussion should be obvious by now, but let's spell it out. We are speaking here of *Montreal Main* as a queer classic, and yet the subject matter of the film includes a relationship that has been excised from queer. The film occupies a paradoxical position of being simultaneously queer and not queer, both counting and not counting, both representing and not representing. Far from being legitimated as a queer subject by this paradox, the relationship of Frank and Johnny fundamentally challenges the entire basis of queer that emerged in the very late 1980s as a resistance to the identity politics of "lesbian" and "gay," terms which in various ways had become too normative for radicals as they mainstreamed.

The shared reticence both of old-school lesbian and gay activists who view(ed) the world more or less categorically along lines of identity and the queer theorists whose bread and butter is busting up conceptual and political boundaries points to the challenge of interpreting *Montreal Main* as a queer film. The film is an orphan because it was abandoned—not because its parents died. The atmosphere of practical and theoretical indifference, disgust, and rejection of the issues raised by Frank and Johnny's relationship inflects our interpretation of the film. Let me ask the reader a series of defining questions. Is Johnny a boy, or a teen? Is he pubescent or pre-pubescent? Is Frank bisexual, gay, a homosexual, a boy lover, or a pedophile? These definitions, were they to be established in advance, would shape the boundaries of what we could say and what we could not say.

One possibility is to read away from the relationship of Frank and Johnny and focus on the queer milieu as a product of a legitimately gay historical subculture. That is not as absurd as it sounds. Steven Alan Carr wrote about the film *L.I.E.* (Michael Cuesta 2001), ignoring the matter of intergenerational sexuality and focusing instead on the young teen character Howie's Jewish-inflected sexuality, from which Carr claims, without a touch of irony, "one traditionally looks away" (Carr 2005, 316). Avoiding the obvious, an author can make hay with the backdrop. Certainly *Montreal Main* lends itself to such a reading as its backdrop is fascinating, and the film, in fact, has endured a number of avoidant readings. This approach would save us much grief but only by denying the challenge of the film. Why should this challenge be denied when it is full to overflowing with political and cultural relevance?

Let's say we accept intergenerational sexuality as the centerpiece of the film. There remain many choices. Let's examine two.

If we insist on the pubescence of Johnny—even though he exhibits no overwhelming signs—we might be able to avoid the question of pedophilia altogether. Frank would not be interested in a prepubescent boy, but in an adolescent boy, a teenager with all the rights to sexual curiosity and to the question of teen sexuality that lingers on the margins of LGBTQ political discourse. *Montreal Main* would come alive politically because of the limits we place on it. It would become a defensible, albeit challenging, revival of a question that many in the LGBTQ world privately admit continues to perplex and concern them. What is foreclosed, however, is a discussion of what I think is shown on the screen: a relationship between a man and a boy. Johnny's unbroken voice, the hairlessness of his face and legs, and his slight frame do not point to a longstanding encounter with puberty.

If we accept that and take Johnny to be a boy, a pre- or barely pubescent twelve-year-old boy, then Frank qualifies for a psychiatric diagnosis of pedophilia, and all the difficult politics and history start pouring in, the existential perspective that views pedophilia not merely as an outlier sexuality outside the fold of legitimate queer politics but as the charged slander of the enemies of queer, the very idea that undermines queer legitimacy. What is foreclosed, for many people, is an LGBTQ reading of *Montreal Main*: Frank is not one of us.

What a mess. Does Johnny not lead us precisely to the boundary of acceptable political and cultural discourse? Why not accept this as our task—to occupy this frontier territory and tease out its complications? Or shall we take up our distinctions in order to avoid opening a discussion? Have we said enough on the subject of intergenerational sexuality?

Easy distinctions are had at a cheap price only for those who stand at a distance, where one can ignore their political effects. The Franks of the world are stuffed into the same sex offender registries and the same civil commitment centers, and are the targets of the same vigilantes and barely restrained police forces that target the baby rapers. The Johnnys of the world are infantilized as assuredly as three-year-olds. These moves obscure the fact the individuals caught up in these easy distinctions are living in a political and cultural apocalypse. We abandon the question of pedophilia and the child at a cost.

If pedophilia has risen up as an ethereal specter, ever-present and ever-absent, a creature of the shadows that dominates us with fear, then the child has also risen up, the theological good to pedophilia's demonological evil (Davies 2007, 378; Berlant 2004, 67). And if we agree to provisionally accept this point as a beginning, the reader will see how narrative functions beyond or beside the directly empirical, the real actual fact of sexual abuse or child sexuality or teen sexuality or pedophile sexuality. Pedophilia and the child become ahistorical containers of real and imagined grievances, fears, hopes, and dreams; abstractions rather than concrete events and experiences.

This abstraction animates enormous cultural forces that power institutional and state power grabs, targeting not only our favorite enemies but increasingly the population at large. For example, the UK now registers citizens who are *not* "pedophiles." The Independent Safeguarding Authority (*isa-gov.org.uk*), originally a list intended to vet teachers and caregivers, will now also include upward of eleven million Britons with incidental exposure to children in their work—the authority's vague reassurances notwithstanding. The European Union is pushing for Internet data-retention laws that would warehouse everyone's emails and Google searches, selling the idea as a fight against online child pornography (Engström 2010). Today, the paranoia runs so deep, English football referees have refused "to shake the hands of young players for fear of being accused of child abuse" (*East Anglian Times* 2007) and "men are advised" by "community safety officers" of the Safe Child Scheme in Wales, UK, not to approach children for "fear they may be branded as child abusers" (Men 2009). UK hobby clubs "are now closing their doors to young people ... because of the mountain of checks and paper-work" now required to keep children safe (Bennett 2007). These are institutional and cultural developments worth critiquing, and this can only be accomplished if we allow ourselves to address the dichotomy that is producing so much fear.

Consider how different it is for the other *idée fixe*, terrorism and the terrorist, which critical people intuitively understand needs to be queried because of the danger of unlimited expansion of state and private powers. The idea that we could or should avoid examining the political issue of pedophilia is a deeply disturbing occlusion of queer and radical politics, one that obscures the workings of some of the great political and social changes of our times, both on the local and global level. Two of the most urgent concerns of our society are our battles with the terrorist (an enemy without, sometimes found within) and the pedophile (the enemy within, sometimes found without). Both nodes resonate with fear and panic. Both produce an ever-increasing panoply of surveillance and "wars" that seek to eliminate their enemies. Such is the specter of the pedophile that we excuse the excesses of anti-pedophile measures. A critical review revives the questions that were foreclosed by the term "pedophile" and doesn't simply rephrase and reinforce the language of the narrative of abuse and its categories, which functions to obliterate all criticism.

It has become necessary to speak directly to the specter of the pedophile that circulates around this film—and around our culture. It is simply not possible to talk about *Montreal Main* without talking about pedophilia. The pedophile, the central figure of the abuse narrative, is a conceptual black hole devouring everything in its vicinity—ephebophile, pederast, boy lover, minor-attracted adult, child lover—so that no alternative concept can operate to produce alternative meanings. All these terms reduce to pedophile, with no perceived remainder. We therefore continually and necessarily return to the figure of the pedophile whenever relationships like Frank and Johnny's make their appearance.

The health of a culture depends a great deal on possessing multiple narratives, different readings, each of which has something to offer. Multiple overlapping and competing narratives produce the conditions for complexity and nuance, where otherwise simplicity dominates, masking other ways of thinking and experiencing. The abuse narrative is one possible narrative circulating in the broader intergenerational category, one we can open up by examining cinema to see alternate ways of thinking and processing events, people, and feelings. *Montreal Main* provides an important intervention here because it came at a time before either the politicized and entitled boy-love consciousness, or the abyss of the anti-pedophile sexual abuse narrative made their demands on us. Frank and Johnny's relationship is not celebrated as a victory, but it isn't condemned either.

Man-boy cinema
Straight cinema often produces man-boy relations that are cartoonish, for example Christopher Lloyd's Doc to Michael J. Fox's Marty McFly in *Back to the Future* (Robert Zemeckis, 1985); or the cute and astute *Fido* (Andrew Currie, 2006), which positioned a friendly zombie as a "queer" other to a young boy (Kesun Loder). Other times, these relations are defined by rigid categories of father-son (*Anche libero va bene* [*Libero*], Kim Rossi Stuart, 2006), other relative (*Mon Oncle*, Jacques Tati, 1958), teacher (*Les Choristes*, Christophe Barratier, 2004), or abuser.

When mainstream cinema takes up the tropes of the abuse narrative, such as in the Sean Penn vehicle *Mystic River* (Clint Eastwood, 2003) or *The Woodsman* (Nicole Kassell, 2004) starring Kevin Bacon, it occasionally twists them for dramatic effect (Davies 2007). Probably the most infamous was the purportedly autobiographical *The Heart Is Deceitful Above All Things* (Asia Argento, 2004), a film that depicted a young boy as a victim of the physical, emotional, and sexual abuse of the adults around him. *Heart*'s supposedly male author, JT Leroy, was unmasked as a female fraud without an abuse history, proving the memoir genre had devolved into a form of vile child pornography, with an audience that preferred images of violence to those of pleasure and friendship.

What does "queer" have to offer boys in the post-exclusion era? Journalist and activist Bill Andriette says, "Not much," in this rather sharply worded commentary:

> The broad, longstanding anthropological baseline
> is that boys are socialized by being brought into the
> male group, with men who have an erotically charged
> fondness for them offering openings and footholds.
> Across times and cultures, older males' desire for
> boys appears a broad, albeit variable and repressible,
> tendency; in the present-day West, under conditions
> of supreme censure, [it is] now evident only in
> those for whom the feelings are strongly marked.
> Such is evident from any account of homosexuality
> addressing its biological, cross-species, and cross-
> cultural basis and expression—such as James Neill's
> *The Origins and Role of Same-Sex Relations in Human
> Societies* (McFarland & Co., 2009).

By the time "queer" had become its own subculture, this basic pattern has already been somewhat disrupted. Queers offer young males money for sex, a place to crash in time of need, attention from those more established, or just sexual release, rather than entrée into male society (i.e., in most times and places, into society *per se*). As well, queers offer more specialized goods: at the artistic high-end, erotically tinged mentor/apprentice relations help [the] transfer of cutting edge knowledge and sensibility.

But as queer becomes (as now) just an empty pseudo-oppositionary tendency or brand, a temporary mode of protest among a slice of the privileged, then queer has nothing to offer boys. And indeed, boys stay utterly away, making "gay" or "queer" the essential present-day Western juvenile taunts.

Montreal Main is a document from the end of that middle period, when the question you asked could still be posed and not simply answered in the negative. (Andriette 2010)

If queers have nothing to offer boys, man-boy relations in queer films ought to be anemic, reproducing or negotiating around dominant norms as a way of masking their failure to contribute anything over and above heteronormative notions of child-rearing. From the perspective of sexual minorities who are attacked and controlled by these norms, queer cinema will appear to be complicit with the dominant culture as it takes care to avoid dangerous conflicts. Although not all queer cinema reinforces these norms, as we shall see in the discussion of man-boy cinema, it's important to briefly point to examples that do.[23] In the post-exclusion era, queer cinema often negotiates around both adults desiring younger people and younger people desiring older people, either by neutralizing desire or displacing it into a threatening character who by definition cannot be gay. Let's briefly review three gay films that reinforce the norm, each in their own way.

A Very Serious Person (Charles Busch, 2006) avoids investigating dangerous man and boy themes, though it superficially dabbles in them. *Very Serious* is a recommendable,

---

23. For reasons of space, many films could not be addressed. Todd Haynes's depth has enabled him to address the abuse narrative obliquely (*Poison*, 1991) and a perverse child sexuality directly (*Dotty Gets Spanked*, 1993). *Ang pagdadalaga ni Maximo Oliveros* (*The Blossoming of Maximo Oliveros*, Auraeus Solito, 2005) speaks directly of man-boy relations with openness and complexity. The film adaptation of Augusten Burrough's *Running with Scissors* (Ryan Murphy, 2006) mines the comedic and pathetic potentials of man-boy relations from a boy's perspective. Most important, perhaps, is Gus Van Sant's *Paranoid Park* (2007), which I interpret as a love poem to adolescence. And Todd Solondz qualifies as a queer of sorts, with his multiple stabs at deconstructing pedophilia, child sexuality, and gender in *Welcome to the Dollhouse* (1998), *Happiness* (2001), and *Palindromes* (2004) (Davies 2007, 378).

good-natured, low-budget feature exploring gay identity generationally divided between twelve-year-old Gil (P.J. Verhoest) and Jan (queer performance star and director Busch), a fortysomething gay male nurse in charge of Gil's dying aunt and legal guardian. The film develops a paternal but not pederastic theme. The drama is not situated around sexual initiation. The only scene that plays with the erotic potential between the man and boy sees Gil slowly sidle up to Jan on his bed as he quizzes him about being gay, an intimacy abruptly cut off by the uptight Jan, who shoos Gil out of his room. Instead, Jan serves as gatekeeper to gay culture—fashion, ballet, a gay-friendly hair and nails salon, and other counter-masculine pursuits—which helps initiate the becoming-gay child into an alternate manhood.

After a series of comings-out and pedagogic moments, the film closes with a drama around whether Jan will adopt the newly orphaned boy, which the film resolves clumsily in the negative. A gay man may want a child, but the legally orchestrated heterosexual family remains the proper place for a child, even a gay one.

Whole New Thing (Amnon Buchbinder, 2005) helps develop a stronger distinction between the world of child and adult, whether gay or straight. Early in the film, the adolescent Emerson (Aaron Webber) develops a crush on his gay teacher Don (played by another icon of gay cinema and co-scriptwriter Daniel MacIvor), and through precocious charm lures him into the sauna. But Don resists the boy's

FIGURE 26. Teacher Don tries to ignore what Emerson is thinking in *Whole New Thing*. DVD cover art © 2008 Picture This!

advances and is firmly established by the film as a man lover. Never are we in doubt about his purely professional motivations toward the boy. In another case of clumsy endings, Emerson runs away and stumbles upon a boy-loving man in a toilet cruising spot, only to be lured to a threatening situation. Youthful gay desire is tempered by the recognition of the supposed truth that any man who mirrored that desire back to him would be abusive, cruel, and utterly selfish. Gay identity is re-secured as not-pederastic by Don's rescue of Emerson, returning him into the loving arms of a gay tolerant nuclear family. And they all lived happily ever after.

Finally, *Mysterious Skin*, by acclaimed queer filmmaker Gregg Araki (2004), moves gay identity into perfect synchronicity with anti-pedophile hysteria. The film opens with eight-year-old Neil (played by ten-year-old Chase Ellison) having sex with his little league coach, played by the handsome actor Bill Sage. The sex is portrayed with overblown aesthetics—colorful children's cereal flying into the air and raining down—distancing the viewer. Later, we see Neil masturbating. Because for the bulk of the film the child sex is presented as essentially non-threatening, the audience might be forgiven for thinking the boy enjoyed his experiences. Fast forward ten years, and Neil (now played by Joseph Gordon-Levitt) is a cocky gay prostitute living on the edge, turning rough tricks, being tracked by unstable age-mate Brian (Brady Corbet), who sees in Neil a possible explanation for his UFO abduction memories.[24]

It is revealed later in the film that Neil lured the slightly younger Brian (George Webster) into sex with his coach. Although the child sex has until this moment been depicted as pleasant enough, and something Neil actively participated in, the final scenes of the film show how twisted it really was: Brian's memories of alien experiments mask his real experience of fisting the coach.

Neil's confidence in his childhood sexual experience is based on a lapse of memory that masked the true nature of the events whose corrosive powers left him with nothing but a "black hole heart," a recovered memory narrative typical of the 1990s. This late recognition—or reconceptualization—ultimately neutralizes the value of the man-boy relation, revealing it to be nothing but a contamination of gay male identity. The becoming-gay child has been misled by the too-queer adult; that-which-lies-beyond-the-heterosexual destroying access not only to heteronormativity but

---

24. *Mysterious Skin* was based on the 1995 novel of the same name by Scott Heim, who explains the genesis of his novel, "I realized that someone speaking under hypnosis about what they thought was a UFO abduction was so similar to the things people say when they're under hypnosis remembering sexual abuse memories" (Lee 2005). See Susan Clancy's book *Abducted* (Harvard University Press, 2005) for a fine introduction to the recovered memory debate.

homonormativity as well, leaving Neil a failed homosexual, prone to self-destructive excess.

That this excess is narrativized by an act of fisting, that twisted pedagogical moment of the film in which the coach teaches Neil how to take it too far, is not insignificant. Fisting is not, to my knowledge, in the repertoire of boy lovers, but a practice that emerged from the androphile underground, the most extreme form of penetration. For that reason, I believe *Mysterious Skin* is really a confrontation between man-boy sexuality and gay male sexual extremes. Subterranean, not-for-Oprah homosexual "excesses" are morphed onto the androphile's worst nightmare, his doppleganger, the boy lover, who acts as scapegoat to carry the moral weight that endangers all gay men in the era of AIDS.

Mysterious Skin is masterful in many ways, but by giving the audience just what it expected all along—trauma—it fails to explicate the truly dangerous man-boy situation: the one that leaves us questioning. After all, how can skin be *mysterious* when we assume we can predict its outcomes?

We have seen how "gay" serves as a neutralizing perspective which avoids challenging the abuse narrative, inscribing old norms with a shiny new political identity. So positioned, we know what to expect. "Gay" that has nothing to do with the aesthetics of the boy shall not be disrupted by his appearance; the boy, who has nothing to do with the adult, shall not be disrupted by the appearance of the gay man. Once these grounds are established, conventional gay male identity can negotiate the parental, pedagogic, and even the potentially erotic, unmolested, so to speak, by the specter of the pedophile.

The cartoonish and rigid categories of straight cinema give the general direction for a normative gay cinema that wishes to be uncontaminated by the specter of the pedophile. When the tropes of normative development and sexuality are disrupted narratively, relationships are constructed as threatening. The boy who does not know what he is meets the man who does not know what he wants, and both travel toward something we do not fully understand and can't predict. That is a dangerous man-boy relationship, one that undermines our expectations or inhabits them in unsettling ways.

Cinema that embraces these contradictions and dangers is man-boy cinema. Even films lacking overt erotic and sexual orientation issues can be more challenging to the status quo than mainstream gay cinema because their ambiguity encourages pederastic readings, as in *Møv og Funder* (*Hideaway*, Niels Gråbøl, 1991). After his vacation plans have been canceled by his father, twelve-year-old Møv (Kasper Tuxen) protects a wounded twentysomething criminal on the run, Funder (Allan Winther), whom he transforms by his simple loyalty. Scenes of nudity, sleeping together in the same bed, and the themes of hiding, criminality, and mutual dependence lend themselves to a pederastic reading in ways many contemporary gay films purposefully resist.

But some films are more direct. Probably the most conventionally unsettling is *L.I.E.* The film sets up what the audience expects—the vulnerable young queer Howie (Paul Dano) meets a manipulative sexual predator, Big John (Brian Cox)—then narratively distorts the characters, making the boy stronger than we expect, and the man capable of love. In *Il sapore del grano* (*The Flavor of Corn*, Gianni Da Campo, 1986[25]), the boy Duilio (Marco Mestriner) pursues a relationship with his teacher Lorenzo (Lorenzo Lena), who must grapple with his feelings of love and friendship. In Arthur J.Bressan's *Abuse* (1983), a conventional story about child familial abuse is inverted when gay filmmaker Larry (Richard Ryder) finds a "star" for his child abuse film, thirteen-year-old Thomas (Raphael Sbarge), and then elopes with him when there appears to be no way to stop the abuse, or otherwise continue their own sexual relationship. Even a film by Mel Gibson, *The Man Without a Face* (1993), can be challenged by a queer character, the figure of McLeod (Mel Gibson), a teacher internally exiled by suspicions of sex with a former student who is lured into a chaste but intimate friendship with twelve-year-old Charles (Nick Stahl).

Montreal Main occupies a middle position in the pantheon of man-boy films, openly handling the sensitive subject, but

---

25. The film is now apparently being repackaged and distributed with the more accurately translated title *The Taste of Wheat* (the crop grown by Duilio's peasant family).

without recourse to an established frame to give it sense, and without demanding a resolution that settles the question. On its surface, *Montreal Main* depicts the relationship between two "straight" males, its erotics configured so subtly the reader might wonder if it is gay at all. What is Frank for Johnny? And what is Johnny for Frank? How is queer reinvested and perhaps reinvented by the encounter between them?

Johnny is a typical boy. He may fit the profile of the androgynous *pueros capillatos* with his long hair and pre- or barely pubertal features unblemished by adolescent overdoses of testosterone, and someone could mistake him for a girl, as indeed Frank does when he discovers Johnny sitting alone in his room reading a magazine, his long hair obscuring his face and frame. But it's important to situate the boy in his era—when androgyny was fashionable and long hair was *de rigueur*. Johnny is not a 1970s gender-bender, but his shy demeanor confounds our expectations about putative masculine drive. He's still a kid, definitely the receptive partner in conversation, utterly overwhelmed in his scenes with fast-talking Steve, who speaks on behalf of both of them. For the bulk of the film, he's along for the ride, and the queer demimonde offers him a sort of welcoming carnival where Johnny can come, connect, get out of the rut of the ordinary, try new things, and see new possibilities.

Frank, while physically masculine and capable of relationships with women, wishes, as Bozo sarcastically puts it "to

know what it's like to be a homo for an hour." Frank stealth-
ily enters Johnny's bedroom from behind a carved African-
style mask. "Boo!" The words never escape Frank's lips as
he retreats in confusion and embarrassment. Frank fails to
perceive Johnny correctly, and the boy unwittingly pranks
Frank with his gender ambiguity, sparking an erotic fascination that carries us through to the end of the film.

That makes it hard to pin down Frank: Is he attracted to
Johnny *qua* the feminine or *qua* boy? Frank is established as
not determinately straight or gay, and this ambiguity under-
writes the tension of the entirely inarticulate eroticism of his
relationship with Johnny. What will he do? We don't know,
and Frank doesn't, either.

But the queer question doesn't circulate around Frank's
orientation alone. We must also ask what Johnny wants from
Frank. One theorist has spoken of the role of the pre- and
adolescent crush that links a boy to a man who represents an
ideal to which the boy aspires, the erotic counterpart to the
pedagogical relation. Does Johnny have a crush on Frank?
Does he want to be like him? Crucially, could this inequality
of their intertwining crushes function as a relationship? Can
Frank and Johnny come together?

Confrontations with desire

> Each person has a dream he hopes will come true even
> though it seems impossible. Sometimes it seems like the

> whole world is against you, and more often than not,
> it's true. Like everyone else, I have a dream. One that is
> steady, unchangeable, and which I live in secret.
> —Duilio, *The Flavor of Corn*

As a visual medium, it is no surprise that cinema often articulates desire through observation. One character sees another and is moved somehow by this, drawn into an encounter that changes both of their lives. That is the plot of *Montreal Main* in a nutshell. Seeing a body is a precursor to touching it, the connection apparently so inborn that an image can elicit an immediate physiological response in the viewer. Outside the frame, the audience is moved by what they see and fall in love with a character or a film. There is a name for this: scopophilia, or the love of watching.

In *Du er ikke alene* (*You Are Not Alone*, Ernst Johansen and Lasse Nielsen, 1978), a film that like *Les amitiés particulières* (*This Special Friendship*)[26] traces the love affair of an older teen boy with a barely pubescent boy at a boarding school, we find fifteen-year-old Bo (Anders Agensø) on the beach

---

26. *You Are Not Alone* and *This Special Friendship* articulate the love of barely pubescent boys and the ability of boys to love in return. In both of these films, the younger boys are around twelve years of age, and their paramours are fifteen or sixteen, a difference that raises eyebrows. Such liaisons, like relationships between boys and men, are potentially illegal; adolescents have been put on the sex offender registry for life for love affairs like these.

FIGURE 27. *You Are Not Alone* (1978): Bo wonders what his feelings for Kim mean. DVD still. © Steen Herdel Filmproduktion

lost in thought after catching himself staring at the round behind of his friend. Later he watches hairless twelve-year-old Kim (Peter Bjerg) disrobe in the shower before asking him what he knows about sex. (Apparently, Kim says, it is "wonderful.") In *Voor een verloren soldaat* (*For a Lost Soldier*, Roeland Kerbosch, 1992), a wartime memoir depicting the post-Liberation love affair between Jeroen (Maarten Smit), a twelve-year-old Dutch boy, and Walt (Andrew Kelley), a twentysomething Canadian soldier, there is a scene very similar to the one that opens *You Are Not Alone*: Jeroen examines the naked body of a slightly older boy after they've taken a swim. Later, Jeroen finds Walt naked in the shower and wrestles with him. In all these scenes, a character is given a space to encounter a body visually and time to digest the encounter. The audience understands that something crucial is happening.

But when viewers think about it, Steve's suggestion to Bozo, "Frank's all right, give him time. Let him document it," terrifies them. Almost forty years after the film was made, Frank's request to take Johnny up the Mountain because he's "been taking pictures of kids lately" sets off alarm bells. What was Ann thinking, allowing her son to do this? Today we know so much better, and the events of *Montreal Main* would be preemptively blocked.

On the Mountain, Frank directly encounters Johnny as an erotic object during an afternoon of photography and play that initiates their relationship. Frank's gaze takes grotesque cinematic form lurching over Johnny's face from above; there is a startling cut to Frank's sweaty panic in his bed alone. Both Frank and the audience are innocent of everything but an awareness of the impulse to take this interest one step further. Frank's unsettling recognition of his power to produce this turn of events—to produce this apparent victim—closes hereafter the erotic shutter of Frank's camera within the film.

A similar moment of sexual panic and disavowal is found in *The Flavor of Corn*. Lorenzo, the young teacher, has gradually opened his heart to twelve-year-old Duilio, after a period of visits to the boy's home and exchanged gifts. On his last visit, Duilio holds Lorenzo's hand and kisses him on the

FIGURE 28. Victim? Johnny looking up into the desiring lens. DVD still.

mouth. The next day in class, Lorenzo smiles at Duilio, then passes his eyes across the room. He sees a boy observing an older boy of seventeen. Lorenzo notices the older boy stroking his erect penis through his tight jeans. The younger boy takes an interest in this, from which the older boy finds some satisfaction. Lorenzo snaps: "Get out! Animal!" When the older student leaves, the camera pans back into the room, finding all the students dumbfounded and Duilio looking angry.

In this scene, Lorenzo is confronted with an analogue of the desire circulating between himself and Duilio. He *is* the older boy pleasuring himself in the sexual awareness of the younger boy. The tender embraces, the gifts exchanged, and family suspicions negotiated—which the plot heretofore subtly narrated—give way to the explicit lust of the older boy's engorged member and the erotic trance of the younger boy who does not appear either afraid or uninterested.

Similarly, Frank's dream—of what?—is disrupted by seeing his desire reflected in/by the camera lens. Frank dreams, perhaps, about Johnny as a passive recipient of his attentions, rather than a participant, and he fears taking any further steps, not knowing what he might do or become. This man, who snooped through the Sutherlands' dresser drawers and wallets, may be more curious than he has a right to be, but he's no thief.

The pedophile gaze

Montreal Main does not fence in its eroticism. Johnny is established as something beautiful and erotic not only for Frank, but for the audience as well. The film does not only tell us what Frank sees as beautiful, it tells us what is beautiful: Johnny. In the family breakfast scene, we are supplied a close-up shot of his thick lips as he sucks down his orange juice. The video pre-shoot editor wondered about "the succulent close-ups of young Johnny's full-lipped mouth cut into a dinner sequence [*sic*] where Vitale the character is not present, leaving Vitale the filmmaker to explain just whose point of view those luscious [close-ups] are from?" (Michaelson 1974, 39). The mise-en-scène sets up Johnny's lips as an out-of-place fragment and fails to fully determine the scene as a reality or as Frank's dream. Perhaps it is the dream of the film audience.

Raising the stakes, just before Johnny escapes his home to go on his night-time bike ride, he is shown in close-up getting out of bed in his tight white briefs, coming down the stairs, and putting his clothes on while sitting on the back steps of his home. (Amplified in the video pre-shoot, this sequence included even more of Johnny getting out of bed.) The boy's body is on display: pale, thin, tautly muscular, hairless. What is the purpose of focusing the camera on this? We assume Frank is interested—but he is not there. We, the audience, observe Johnny in Frank's place. If we desire Johnny, we multiply Frank's desire for him; even if we don't, the pedophile gaze is within us.

Intergenerational cinema itself establishes scopophilic norms for boy lovers. Cinema, and especially digital technology and home theater, provide the audience with the power to invest eroticism in new ways. In the first place, intergenerational cinema is not simply an observation of what exists. It fictionalizes, overlays, and grants us access to realities unattainable here and now, shaping our expectations. Men see how the William Hurt character loves James (Chris Cleary) in the adoption melodrama *Second Best* (Chris Menges, 1994), and they want to love like that. They see how Jeroen in *For a Lost Soldier* loves Walt, and they want to find a boy who is receptive like that. They see boys (Peter Glawson among them) throw off their clothes in *The Genesis Children* (Anthony Aikman, 1972), and want to find boys as carefree as that. The films simultaneously fill a need and elaborate on it.

Where politics or reality fail to fulfill a dream, there remains the purely mechanical reproduction of the body of the boy. With DVD freeze-frames, a body is available for exacting inspection. Was that well-hung boy Pasquale (Francesco Casisa) from *Respiro (Grazia's Island*, Emanuele Crialese, 2002) circumcised? Study the nude scene of the same actor in *Nuovomondo* (*The Golden Door*, Crialese, 2006). Want to get a better look at the character Reine (Tomas Fryk) in *Barnens ö (Children's Island*, Kay Pollak, 1980)? Replay it in slow motion. What was under Jack's (Chris Furrh's) loincloth during the fight scene with Ralph (Balthazar Getty) in *The Lord of the Flies* (Harry Hook, 1990)? Freeze the frame to find out.

Intergenerational, coming-of-age, and boy-related cinema provides a wide body of work that has not yet been suppressed by the censorship apparatus, a corpus through which pedophilic and pederastic desire can operate, draw out of it what it can, and fulfill itself in fantasy, compelling narrative, and visual stimulation. But this non-contact cinematic eroticism is not greeted benignly. What is at issue is "pedophile" desire itself not any supposed harm it may do. What is to be eradicated is desire, not harm.

There was a time in cinema—between two eras of censorship, the Hollywood Production Code that sputtered out in the 1960s and the institutionalization of politically correct panic during the 1990s—in which youthful nudity was not only acceptable but almost expected. In addition to anomalous Ur-films like *Zéro de conduite* (Jean Vigo, 1933), many coming-of-age films from the late 1960s to the early '90s, often from European countries, feature the skin of youth.[27]

27. A list including *You Are Not Alone*, *La discesa di Aclàs Floristella (Aclà*, Aurelio Grimaldi, 1972) *Uroki v kontse vesny (Lessons at the End of Spring*, Oleg Kavun, 1989), *For a Lost Soldier*, *Vito e gli altri (Vito and the Others*, Antonio Capuano, 1991), *Pelle erobreren (Pelle the Conqueror*, Billie August, 1987), *Kes* (Ken Loach, 1969), *Le souffle au coeur*, *Pixote: A Lei do Mais Fraco (Pixote*, Hector Babenco, 1981), *Lord of the Flies (*Peter Brook, 1963 and Harry Hook, 1990*), *The Hideaway*,

This cinema was not always innocent of its erotic potentials. As mentioned, both *You Are Not Alone* and *For a Lost Solder* depict eroticized adolescent and pre-adolescent nudity. Both *Barnen's ö* and *Novecento* (*1900*, Bernardo Bertolucci, 1976) feature arousal. Although artistic merit is no longer a reliable defense—in fact, not at all in some jurisdictions—cultural prestige and artistic alibis continue to exact pressure, and these two films are available at your local video store. On the other hand, *Maladolescenza* (Pier Giuseppe Murgia, 1977), a film featuring explicit nudity and sexual acts between an adolescent boy and two twelve-year-old girls, has not fared so well and received the death sentence of a child pornography classification by the German government in 2006.

Today the child's body in cinema is a censored body. In P.J. Hogan's *Peter Pan* (2003), the rear ends of two boys caught in a tree were digitally generated and the nudity of a boy in a bathtub was digitally erased to block the pedophile freeze-frame. (This is somewhat ironic, given that the author of the original play, J.M. Barrie, was very likely a boy lover himself.[28]) In *Romulus, My Father* (Richard Roxburgh,

---

Ti kniver i hjertet (*Cross my Heart and Hope to Die*, Marius Holst, 1994), *The Genesis Children, Benny's Video* (Michael Haneke, 1992), *Dreamspeaker, Emperor Tomato Ketchup* (*Tomato Kecchappukôtei*, Shuji Terayama, 1971), and *Ba wang bie ji* (*Farewell My Concubine*, Chen Kaige,1993) barely scratches the surface.

28. A recent biography (Birkin 2003) suggests Barrie altered the will

2007), we observe a strange scene of mother and son (Kodi Smit-McPhee) "bathing" together while clothed in a bathtub. Smit-McPhee, is found, clothed again, bathing in *The Road* (John Hillcoat, 2009) while his father, played by Viggo Mortensen, bathes nude. Even though they are absolutely alone in a desolate world, the boy cannot disrobe, and instead risks pneumonia by dampening his underclothes. This reverses the logic of revealing the child body found in *Montreal Main* in the breakfast and dressing scenes. Instead of the non-diegetic eroticization of 1974, we find illogical prudery in 2009.

And yet, in *The Road*, parts of "the boy's" body are exposed during a bathing scene that "the man" remembers, the context of memory emphasizing the symbolic importance of the naked child. We see his knobby knees, his bare shoulders, and back as he is bathed by his mother, in a memory of home and hearth long obliterated at this point in the film. Child skin is something available in the home under parental supervision, indeed as the act of parental care, but in the cold and barren outside world of moral cannibals—read pedophiles—disrobing is a sin.

Compare this with a scene in *The Hideaway*, where, after sleeping together in the same bed with twelve-year-old Møv, twentysomething Funder, pained by an infected knife wound he sustained at a bar across the street, heads to the

---

of the Llewellyn-Davies boys' mother in order to obtain custody.

bathroom for a shower. Møv joins him. Both are naked in the shower. Funder has pubic hair, and Møv has none. Møv has the body of a child: growing, sexual, asexual, undeveloped, developing, vulnerable, sprightly, physical, beautiful. Why shouldn't we see Møv in all these ways?

There is something that calls us all in the nude child, whether it is in the symbol of the infant Christ or the Freudian turns of Jorodowsky's filial nudity in *El Topo* (Alejandro Jodorowsky, 1970). The naked bodies of children have a meaning for us that circulates somewhere in the domain of pedophilia, but is not entirely captured there. We're invested in this child, now concrete, now abstract, whether we look or not or busy ourselves with policing the boundary. In the past, we simply observed; today, we're not allowed to look, but we often do, anyway.

This looking is overlaid by a hysterical magnification of the pedophile gaze so that it becomes impossible to view the child body as non-sexual and impossible to conceive of this sexuality as anything other than deranged. To ward off the "evil eye" that peers a little too closely, we peer a little too closely, until we see what "they" see. The panicked pedophile gaze of the ever-vigilant is so penetrating—like those cheap X-ray glasses from the comic books—it sees right through clothes, detecting sex and gratification in the most timid pose. Whether at the beach, in the street, or even at school functions, everyone has been robbed of the pleasure of watching children. The pedophile gaze has invaded and implanted itself in the mind of every adult, and we are all suspects. Or, should I say, all men are suspects?

It is no accident that it is the image at stake. Pedophilia, child sexual abuse, and child sexuality itself have theological dimensions. It is the icon of the child that is being defended when the pedophile gaze is attacked. This gaze is made monstrous and demonic by the forces of purity. It is the "animal" of Lorenzo's student engorged by lust, inviting the same in any curious boy it can attract, or the one-sided optic of Frank's camera, leering down on helpless Johnny. Declared an enemy of the child, this way of seeing must be obliterated, without asking too many questions. Rich descriptions give way to ideology on both sides: the purely lust-driven assimilate young bodies as functional opportunities, as holes to be penetrated; the purely puritan assimilate them as sacred grounds where pleasure cannot and never will exist.[29] Neither, in their opportunism, accepts the guidance of a boy's opinion or sways to the gentle vibration of youth.

---

29. Leigh Goldstein (2009) points to how the pedophile gaze is used to control child and teen sexuality. The pedophile gaze is an "ever present and quasi-voracious pedophiliac audience ... [a] predatory, if hypothetical consumer ... constructed as an adult ... [allowing] those who advocate shielding minors from sexually explicit materials to designate a figure of danger who is not the ostensibly innocent child ... displacing the threat of danger away from the [child] producer onto an unspecified and unintended consumer ... avoiding the contradictory position of explicitly vilifying those who[m] they seek to protect."

Failures of communication

> It's an illusion, you keep it out of your reach.
> —Steve, *Montreal Main*

Few films engage the gaze like *Death in Venice*, relying almost entirely on glances between characters to explore the attractions and dangers of the beauty of the boy. Dirk Bogarde plays the spiritually exhausted elder musician Gustav von Aschenbach on a rest-holiday at a Venetian hotel who finds himself entranced by the adolescent beauty of Tadzio, played by an androgynous Björn Andrésen. The audience spends most of the film watching Aschenbach watch Tadzio. Late in the film, Aschenbach attempts to leave cholera-infected Venice but is foiled by the inconvenience of lost luggage, which he deliriously interprets as a stroke of good luck. Instead of warning Tadzio's family of the impending medical disaster, the man returns to his hotel room and stands by the window overlooking the beach, where he sees Tadzio walking far below. And then Aschenbach waves at him and smiles strangely.

But who is Aschenbach waving to? Tadzio neither notices nor returns the man's gesture, and suddenly the viewer is aware of a fresh interpretation running through the film; although the boy has, from the beginning, been seen by the man to be opaquely returning his glances, these may have existed only in the mind of Aschenbach all along. Unlike in

Montreal Main

the novella, Visconti directs his adolescent actor[30] to return the gaze of the man. But this mirroring does not clarify the relationship. Instead, it produces for Aschenbach an ever deepening erotic illusion, which his spiritual sickness cannot untangle. The man, it turns out, is only waving to himself, consumed by depths he mistakenly attributes to the boy. Tadzio, whether he notices Aschenbach or not, is simply material for the artist's final tragic creation as he is extinguished by cholera and the beauty that destroys.

This is not the only reading of *Death in Venice* possible— even within this authorial team (see also Waugh 1993)—but it does fit rather well with the "common-sense" attitudes toward pederast desire, i.e., that it is one-sided, unreciprocated, and therefore emotionally meaningless on top of being morally and psychically dangerous. Boy lovers are just so many Aschenbachs, waving at their illusions.

Montreal Main, too, raises the issue of the emptiness of the erotic gesture toward the boy when Frank asks Johnny the Big Question up in the loft late in the film:

> Frank: "Do you ever think, like, I don't know, like,
> you know Bozo and I are older and everything, you

---

30. Björn Andrésen was sixteen when the film was made. Thomas Mann's 1912 novella of the same name tells us that Tadzio is fourteen. Mann biographer Anthony Heilbut uncovered the true identity of the boy who caught Mann's eye, a young Polish royal, and found he was eleven years old when Mann met him.

183

know, why we're friends, why we like somebody like you? Do you ever wonder what kind of people we are?"

Johnny, smiling: "I don't know."

What is the meaning of this "I don't know?" In a way, because *Montreal Main* featured non-professional actors, the best scenes with Johnny are all miscommunications, the boy providing us with his "real" reaction, unmediated by concept of character. As Vitale put it: "[A]ll the emotions are real ... based on [the actors] themselves. It's like type-casting. Basically I don't believe in acting" (Michaelson 1974, 13). In an interview in 2009, John Sutherland told me he often didn't know what was going on or what they would do each shooting day. Johnny's grinning purity of performance probably means, "I don't know, Frank, I'm just standing here because you told me to."

But narratively it means, "I don't know what motivates you, Frank." We know Frank is fishing for awareness on Johnny's part, and coming up empty-handed. He wants to know if Johnny is wise: "Do you know I'm gay for you, Johnny? Do you know we can play at more than electricity?" But Johnny is not wise, and Frank quickly abandons his attempt, the questions pressing him back into obscurity.

This "I don't know" is an epistemological countersign to every erotic encounter between men and boys, a socially constructed demand for determination in advance. The man asks, "Do you want to make it?" and the boy responds with—no matter what he actually says—"I don't know." It doesn't matter what he does or does not actually know or want. The "I don't know" is culturally inscribed as essential to the being of the boy—and consequently, he does not want, either. For how can a person want what they do not know?

Not every film treats boys as utterly naïve. Fifty-four years before *Montreal Main*, John Ford's *Just Pals* (1920) recognized the sexual knowledge of young Bill (George Stone), the street kid that homeless Bim (Buck Jones) takes under his wing. When Bill asks his older friend Bim whether they should "cop a feel" of a girl nearby, Bim scolds him, since that is not how to treat a lady. In *Murmur of the Heart*, the boy character Laurent (Benoît Ferreux) is a veritable teen stud, "bagging" not only a female prostitute, but a teen girl and even his own mother. In the soft-core *Private Lessons* (Alan Myerson, 1981), a fifteen-year-old boy (Eric Brown) spies on and is happily seduced by his maid (Sylvia "Emmanuelle" Kristel), eventually making it with her in a bathtub scene. *Léolo* (Jean-Claude Lauzon, 1992) probably takes the cake with its depiction of a twelve-year-old voyeuristic masturbator (Maxime Collin) obsessed with fantasies involving his older female neighbor. We could go on but even Johnny of *Montreal Main* is not entirely devoid of sexual knowledge. Just before Frank picks up Johnny for their adventure on the Mountain, we see Johnny with Tony and his other friends rapping about girls. Tony says: "John knows Janice intimately. He's a Don Juan, crawling with girls." Adolescent bravado aside, Johnny knows something of what he is not supposed to know. Johnny is both Don Juan and ambassador of sexual innocence.

We are led to believe that heterosexual knowledge always comes first in childhood socialization and is most secure and certain. Perhaps this supposed certainty is produced by the straight world to prop up the feared decline of the family or by the queer community to have an enemy to rebel against (heteronormativity). Hetero initiation is always confusing, but easy; homo is terrifying and requires a miracle. These assumptions alone have a way of neutralizing knowledge of homosexuality, making it less sure, reducing its legitimacy. In the oppressive halls of the church-run boarding school of *This Special Friendship*, twelve-year-old Alexandre (Didier Haudepin) asks sixteen-year-old Georges (Francis Lacombrade), "Do you know the thing you're not supposed to know?" meaning homosexuality, the ever-present but never-spoken-of threat in the all-male subculture. Somehow they both know what they are not supposed to know, but the authority of the interdiction means the lovers cannot act upon their knowledge—and isn't that really the point?[31]

---

31. But what if they did? Could Alexandre resist the societal calls to say, "But I didn't know. No, not really!" and refuse to take up the therapeutic narrative and refrain from pointing the finger at Georges as the one who knew better, the one who really failed to obey the rule? Homosexuality may carry the dimension of disavowal when,

The Flavor of Corn illustrates this idea of enforced igno-rance. Early in the film, when Lorenzo is first learning the routines of the school, he receives an essay by a schoolboy who wrote that his sister "bought" her baby. Lorenzo cor-rects this to the verb "to give birth." When this correction comes to the attention of the headmaster, he is, in turn, cor-rected by the headmaster, who tells him, "The verb is sim-ply too realistic." Later Lorenzo asks the boy if he really thinks his sister bought a baby and the boy says he does not. Asked then why he said this, the boy replies, "Because we're in school!" School is a place where the children deceive the adults, and the adults deceive themselves.

Male children of a certain age are chronic masturbators to online pornography, like most adult males ("BJS" 2007; Fidelman 2009). In a single afternoon, every body part and every combination of parts and genders can be uncovered by unclicking "safe search" in Google. Every combination, that is, except those involving youth themselves. This censor-ship does not limit the distribution of child and adolescent orgasm, but merely enables the moral double-think of adults who know young people are sexually aware, yet pay an enor-mous amount of lip service to believing they are sexually

in some narratives, one partner "realizes" it has been a mistake all along. When it happens in age-discrepant relationships, an accusation has the power to destroy the older partner and absolve the younger's "sins." Perhaps what is unknown is not sex at all, but the self: "I don't know if I will turn on you someday."

innocent, incapable of discussion, and utterly incurious, quite unlike we were at those ages. When young people want to know, we deny them knowledge. When they know, we deny their knowledge. When they do, we deny their actions. If we finally accept that young people both know and do, we try to find somebody else to blame.

Children are positioned as victims of online porn, which according to one British newspaper "play[s] on the child's mind," causing them to copy "the images they have seen," and making them "vulnerable to being abused." It is an "inappropriate use of the internet," for children to access pornography online, and any sexual activity young people engage in is merely a misled "copying" of things "they do not have the developmentally [*sic*] capacity to fully comprehend" (*Mail Online* 2007). Following this logic, according to the same report, boys as young as nine are sent for re-education at publicly funded services such as the Warwickshire County Council's Sexualised Inappropriate Behavior Service (SIBS) in the UK when they fool around with each other—to no manifest political opposition from mainstream gay organizations.

In *For a Lost Soldier*, the topic of youthful sexual awareness is handled very well. Jeroen is both aware and unaware of sexuality. After swimming, his friend lies naked beside him, and Jeroen takes the opportunity to observe his body, registering its aesthetic appeal. Later his friend asks him:

Friend: "Do you get a hard-on sometimes?"

Jeroen: "A hard-on? Oh yes ... of course."

Friend: "Liar!"

Although, like his friend, we are unconvinced by Jeroen's claim to knowledge, we are not sure he is entirely innocent either. In the next scene, he caresses his adoptive older brother's side as he sleeps, revealing his desire for skin-on-skin contact. Language also poses an interesting problem in the film as a source of (mis)communication and (mis)understanding. Jeroen, who speaks a fragmentary English he may have learned in school and Walt, who speaks not a word of Dutch, give us wonderful exchanges such as this one:

> Walt: "You have beautiful hands, Jerome [*sic*]. You could be an artist with those hands. You could be a painter or sculptor. When I was your age, we lived in America. We had this neighbor, he was an artist. He always used to say, 'My hands make, but my mind creates.' You're a bit like him."

> Jeroen, fiddling with a rifle: "Shut up. I busy."

Yet, for all its impossibility, an overriding message of the film is how this connection without comprehension puts Jeroen's creative life in motion, a will that is later reborn in the adult Jeroen, who becomes a ballet choreographer.

Walt's admiration of Jeroen's creative potential carries him over somehow to a life in the creative arts. When young Jeroen is tasked by his teacher to write an essay about "What liberation means to me," he immediately brings to mind a fantasy of dance with his adult lover. The older Jeroen seeks to channel this instinctive freedom back into his work.

Sometimes what fails in the domain of language and concepts can find sure footing in the instinctive, the concrete—in touch, dance, sex. In this para-lingual experience of physicality, inscribed by Jeroen's fantasy, the boy was able to take from his experience something of lasting value that guided him throughout his life. Certainly that is not always the case, but can we say it is never the case?

Echoing the conversation between Walt and Jeroen, in *The Flavor of Corn*, Duilio says to Lorenzo, "When I look at you I understand what you say. Even when you don't speak." Mutual understanding is based on something other than being the same age; it depends upon mutual interests and the enjoyment of each other's company. When Duilio and Lorenzo eat at a restaurant, Duilio leads by ordering gnocchi, which Lorenzo orders as well, but with butter sauce. Duilio changes his order to match his friend's. They share a plate of fried fish and a salad. Lorenzo orders white wine, and Duilio takes some as well. Noting this synchronicity, the waiter asks Lorenzo, "Is he your brother?" to which he replies, "Yes." Duilio says to Lorenzo, "Those are the kinds of answers I like."

FIGURE 29. *The Flavor of Corn*: Lorenzo and Duilio relax in the fields. Production still. Courtesy *cvmc.net*.

In *Montreal Main*, communication is foregrounded in the relationship between Bozo and Jackie, which provides a contrasting foil for Frank and Johnny. They talk endlessly; they fight constantly. Bozo and Jackie are of different tribes. Jackie wants stability, reassurances, and probably a middle-class lifestyle. Bozo is freewheeling, inconsistent, and looks down his nose at Jackie's pretensions. No amount of discursive negotiation seems to resolve these issues.

Frank and Johnny are silent together. David Sutherland describes Frank as "so quiet he kinda spooks you a little bit." Johnny, for his part, is seen as a shy observer of the adult world in which he suddenly finds himself, responding monosyllabically and with shrugs and nods to, for example, Steve's barrage of questions. Nearly all of the scenes involving Frank and Johnny are exceptionally quiet: their initial meeting with the mask, their day on the Mountain, their time together at Frank's, as they fiddle with electronics. Only two "real" conversational exchanges occur; the first when Frank asks Johnny the Big Question, and later at the end of the film, when Johnny and Frank argue. It's as if their relationship required as little language as possible and suffered whenever it made its appearance. As with Jeroen and Walt, their relationship is determined by something other than language, a "consent" reached through many small gestures.

Pedagogy and oaths of friendship

Pedagogy is both essential to the relationships between young people and adults, and a way of negotiating desire and making it valuable and productive. Perhaps the supreme pedagogical moment in coming-of-age cinema occurs in *Dreamspeaker*, written by lesbian author Cam Hubert. Peter (Ian Tracey), a twelve-year-old troublemaker with emotional problems, runs away from a boy's reformatory and ends up on the west coast of British Columbia at the cabin of a wise aboriginal elder, the Dreamspeaker (George Clutesi), and his mute friend, whom he met as a boy (Waugh 2006). According to the elder: "I'm not his father by birth, but we've

FIGURE 30. Dreamspeaker and his two "adopted" sons. Production still, from the collection of the Cinémathèque québécoise. © Canadian Broadcasting Corporation

been together a long time. He used to get in a lot of trouble, so I adopted him. Now he's my strength, and I'm his throat." The Dreamspeaker sees Peter as another little troublemaker to care for and takes him under his wing, teaching him the story of Raven, and giving him a place to be.

When the old man suggests Peter try carving, the boy says he can't learn anything. "They did tests and everything," he tells the old man. The Dreamspeaker tells Peter about the old days:

> Old man: "Learning was easier then. Kids didn't sit around all day listening to high-falutin' stuff. You'd let the kid hang around, just watching. If the kid wanted to learn something, you'd show him how it was done. Then one day, you'd give him a try. If he messes it up, it's okay, alright. He was just giving it a try. He wasn't supposed to do [it]. Then, too, everything was done by fours. Four directions, four winds, four seasons to the year, four parts to a tree: roots, trunk, branch, and leaf. So you tell a fellow four times, and it's complete, and he'll never forget."

> Peter: "Wouldn't do any good."

> Old man: "That so?"

> Peter: "Four times, one hundred times, a hundred and four times. Still wouldn't do any good."

Old man: "What wouldn't do any good?"

Peter: "Telling four times."

Old man: "Who'd do that?"

Peter: "You said, 'If you tell him four times he'll never forget.' That's what you said."

Old man: "You learned about four, didn't you?"

In the hands of the master pedagogue, the supposed deficiencies of the boy are challenged and reconfigured, disappearing in a puff of smoke through a different narration. Gone are the categories that limit in advance, replaced by what matters, an act of knowledge.

The Dreamspeaker challenges professional pedagogy with its determinations and replaces it with letting be, giving Peter time and space to unravel himself. The play of vulnerability is essential in bonding between people. We trust—we need to trust—only those to whom we are vulnerable. Peter has to lower his defenses and first accept the validation of the Dreamspeaker before he can develop control over his spirit, the tormenting snake. The Dreamspeaker tricks Peter, not in a way that takes advantage of the boy, but so he opens to himself and recognizes his own value.

Another powerful example of the test of vulnerability is the shaving scene in *L.I.E.* Big John, whom the film has already established to be a bit of an opportunistic creep, finds himself holding a straight razor against the bare neck of fifteen-year-old Howie. This is the same boy who, a few days earlier, he felt up and pressured to watch pornography as he made a one-sided deal to resolve with sex a theft the boy was involved in: "What do you got that's worth a $1,000, hmm? ... You got more than five inches, Howard?" Now, with a razor at the boy's neck, Big John faces a moment of decision. Sensing something of value in his hands, he redeems himself, guiding the blade deftly. Did some spectators expect Big John to slit Howie's throat and bury him in the backyard? In the shadow of pedophilia, the scene, both for the characters and audience, is inevitably all about both desire and danger—powerful precisely because its meanings are doubled. Big John not only makes the right choice, but proves he is something Howie wants, a queer father figure.

Johnny is vulnerable too, and not only to Frank. Throughout the film, the boy is a target of adult influence, from Steve's overwhelming paternalistic raps to his initial meeting with Frank, which was arranged through his mother. Certainly in the eyes of his parents, Johnny is vulnerable to the new adult friends they know too little about, which later leaves Johnny vulnerable to the violence of his father. But this film is especially about how Frank reacts to and flows with Johnny's timid and quiet demeanor. Frank is worried he might go too far, and so is everyone else. But does he?

In the loft, Ann Sutherland's probing question, "fooling

around with what?" is answered by a large spark climbing up two divergent wires, as the pair plays with electrical devices.

Frank: "Oops. Blew a fuse."

Johnny: "Is that from that?"

Frank: "Yeah. It could blow your head off, eh?"

Johnny: "How could it go up those wires then, just those wires?"

Frank: "What do you mean?"

Johnny: "How come it didn't do anything to the wires?"

Frank: "I don't know. Here, you stick your hand in it. I'll set the fuse and we'll try again."

Johnny, smiling: "No."

Frank, smiling: "Okay."

Here, Frank pretends to trick Johnny into endangering himself, which the boy recognizes as a joke. A play on the boy's vulnerability, Frank pushes only to the boundary of Johnny's perception, to what he himself sees as a joke. Frank is sensitive to Johnny's limits, even if he wonders if he'll respect them.

Returning to the Big Question Frank asks Johnny in the

loft, Frank finally decides to go for it, and yet he speaks in subtext the boy isn't yet wise to. Frank refuses to clarify his meaning—to unzip his pants as it were—and have Johnny consider Frank's desire in a direct and unambiguous way. (Compare this with Big John's, "Ever had a blow job?") Frank neither tempts nor pushes Johnny to do anything. In his way, he exemplifies the child liberationist ethos, leaving Johnny to figure things out in his own time, which could be tomorrow, next year, or never. The undemanding quiet uncertainty of the film is carried in the mutual silence of two introverts, quietly passing time with each another in passive pursuits. I sense that Frank would have been patient enough and good enough to Johnny to let their relationship progress like this for years. How many of us as youths had an adult friend like Frank who never crossed the line?

In all these cases, love and eroticism is revealed to possess a sensitivity that resonates at the frequency of the younger partner, particularly in the way it can retract, returning to detumescent friendship, leaving questions unanswered and urges unsatisfied. There is always the question of whether hesitation and sensitivity will be enough. But it is a question: the hesitations and care these older characters develop lay the groundwork for openness to the needs of the boy. Through these moments of vulnerability, closeness may develop, which can be affirmed by oaths of friendship.

Early on, Frank affirms his relationship with Johnny to his friends simply by bringing him along. But this affirma-

tion is never articulated in a scene between Frank and Johnny, except though the regularity of silent play. *Montreal Main*
poses a problem for us in this regard because we track the
relationship to the point where its nascent intimacy, and all
its complications, are just beginning to be felt by Johnny.
The affirmation occurs in the moment of its disavowal: "You
said we were friends!" Then suddenly, they're not.

But we find a number of examples of this kind of friendship in man-boy cinema. Sometimes it is quite an innocent
expectation. When, in *The Hideaway*, Funder and Møv make
an excursion to Funder's apartment, his ex-roommate asks
about Møv.

Roommate: "Who the hell is he?"

Funder: "Just a kid I met in the street."

Møv: "Liar. I've helped you ... You asshole. I hope
you go to jail!"

Funder proves himself to be every bit the shallow user the
audience expected, a sleazy small-time crook tossed about by
people tired of his bullshit. But Møv is taken aback, as if to
say, "I'm not just some kid you found on the street. I'm your
friend!" Møv invests meaning in a relationship Funder views
as merely useful. Ultimately, the boy's faith brings Funder
around, who risks his freedom to save the boy from falling
during a rooftop escape.

A striking and literal example of a ritual affirmation of

FIGURE 31. Ritual affirmation of special friendship through drinking blood. *This Special Friendship*. DVD still. © Jean Delannoy.

friendship occurs in *This Special Friendship*, when the younger boy, Alexandre, proposes to the older Georges, "I'd like us to exchange [blood], so that even if later we don't agree, or act alike, it doesn't matter. 'United forever' this is called."

In this day and age, an oath that overcomes later disagreement is hard to imagine. Perhaps it is performative: when you can conceive of it, and have the courage to say it, it can become true and can carry us over the rivers of doubt and against the dreadful institutions of thought control. Alexandre believed it, claiming defiantly against his priestly oppressors, "Georges and I are one ... we're going to be friends forever ... I'm sure!"

This is England (Shane Mcdonald, 2006) is not a film about man-boy romance, yet it contains such an affirmation. Charismatic thug Combo gets out of prison and attempts to draw his apolitical, adolescent skinhead friends toward the ideology of racist British nationalism. In one scene, prepubescent Shawn throws some punches Combo's way after he opines on the pointlessness of the Falklands War, in which Shawn's father died. Stunned and impressed by the boy's elemental fury, he takes young Shawn under his wing: "Honest, lad, I know how you feel. You ever want anyone to talk to, someone to cry with, or just to fuckin' have a hug or punch the fuck out of, I'm tellin' ya, I'll be there for ya. I won't turn my back on ya. Promise ya that ... I won't let ya down." Like Frank, Combo pulls Shawn into a world of questionable normative value—in this case, away from playfully adolescent destructiveness into the violent para-politics of nationalist skinhead culture from which Shawn is saved only by Combo's inevitable self-destruction. Nevertheless, Combo's oath of friendship is heartfelt.

One rather beautiful affirmation occurs in *The Flavor of Corn*, though it is also deflected, never uttered to the boy who needs to hear it. On the day before he is to leave town forever, Lorenzo passes time with a woman who is, superficially, his girlfriend. He receives a postcard from Duilio.

Girlfriend: "Who is this Duilio? One of your friends?"

Lorenzo: "Yes. Yes, he's my best friend. And he's only twelve years old."

Girlfriend: "He's one of your students?"

Lorenzo: "No. He's someone who taught me everything."

Lorenzo reverses the terms of his engagement with Duilio. He is the student, and the boy is the teacher. What did the boy teach? The power of the "childish illusions" of love, which his girlfriend is too jaded to believe in anymore. Duilio's grandfather, recognizing the special relationship the boy has with his teacher, speaks to the pair at his deathbed, "Professor, he's close to you. He loves you so much. Don't abandon him." Lorenzo nods, but like Frank, ultimately breaks off the friendship.

Somewhere between the empty promises of eternal love men whisper into the ears of women and the taciturn understanding of the hunting pack is the oath of loving loyalty. I wonder what oath would be sufficient to found a boy-love relationship, and whether there is any man who could sustain it in practice. How could this promise be communicated to a boy? Would he believe it when he grew up? And is the oath not also for the boy to make? Yes, but the responsibility lies with the man and society to produce the circumstances that make oaths of friendship sustainable. Men must make promises they can keep, and society must allow them to keep them.

Regardless, Frank never utters such an oath, nor does he even articulate his gratitude for the boy's friendship. Moyle has explained that, at the time, they did not know how to invest psychological depth into their characters (2010). We never hear Frank tell us what he thinks of Johnny. We never hear him speak candidly to Johnny, except, by way of the Big Question, that he and his friends "like someone like" Johnny. Instead, their relationship is a silence, punctuated by silent looks, which we lay interpretations over, according to our own interests, picking up a comment here and an image there to make it say what we want it to say. Just like the Sutherlands, Bozo, Peter, and Steve.

Moralists and preachers

Modern society, with its physical and social mobility, may have enabled homosexual subcultures to dot the straight world, but until very recently, homosexuality has been in confrontation with the moral orders of the day, which always more or less forbade male love. One's moral understanding of homosexuality came first from the preachers who condemned it, knitting with their words the boundaries of social life in the guise of religion and the law.

Today, homosexuality has been divided in two: androphile gay identity and pederastic and pedophile sexualities that are no longer afforded the "defense" of inclusion in gay identity or community. Now as then, the moralists and preachers flood the public space, making broad declarations of the hell and damnation awaiting the sexually divergent. Now as then, secrecy affords the only defense. When the timid, politically unjustified, naïve, and inarticulate fumblings of men and boys, isolated from a supportive social structure, come to the attention of institutions of naming and shaming, the promise of friendship comes under pressure and often shatters. Rarely do we consider the importance of friendships between young people and adults and how they are strengthened and torn apart by cruel social forces. Many PhDs have been written on the negative effects of social opinion on gays and lesbians, but few queers consider how it must feel for boys in relationships with men to carry the weight of social expectations—demands, really—that can distort experiences, replace love with fear and suspicion, and even rewrite history.

There is a moment in *For a Lost Soldier* when Jeroen, along with the audience, thinks the jig is up when his adoptive father confronts him after he has spoken with Walt: "You better come here," says the father. "I've seen it, Jeroen, and I noticed it earlier." Jeroen starts to cry, and bows his head. The father continues: "We're not used to that kind of thing here. Come on ..." Jeroen weeps. "It's wrong to keep the sweets you're given to yourself." The close call fills the boy with the fear and shame of being discovered. His tears absolve him of the wrong crime, and the boy continues to live with his secret, profoundly aware of the priestly warnings to guard against the "lonely and weak moments" of their "brave liberators."

Priestly edicts figure large in *This Special Friendship*, which depicts the highly policed world of the French Catholic boarding school. We hear the priests say at mass, "Beware of your friendships. Let them be pure, your sensibility held firmly in rein. [Pray] that your friendships should be public and friendships of the soul." When Alexandre's love note to Georges ("If your words were caresses, my looks have been kisses") is discovered, the Father Superior says to him, "If you lie to save a friend, it's useless. We know who it concerns. I wish to hear the name from your lips," inviting him to break the oath of friendship.[32] Georges, thinking he can outwit the priests, admits to the relationship, which only opens the pair up to increased pressure.

The priests in *Special* represent moral authority, with their admonitions to beware homosexuality, but they are also bearers of a contradictory morality, enjoying secret nighttime visitations by adolescents. Sometimes this mix is hypocritical, as when Father Trennes says to Georges, "I know who you were dreaming of" and threatens the relationship, later revealed clearly to be a case of "it takes one

---

32. Not unlike Orwell's *1984* where O'Brien uses fear to break Winston Smith and make him repudiate his relationship with Julia.

to know one" when Father Trennes is dismissed for his familiarity with the boys under his care. But even so, the film is, if not sympathetic, tolerant of the contradictory position in which the priest finds himself trapped, reproducing the conditions of his own oppression while bending the rules to the breaking point. It is this very attitude that has been condemned in recent years, shaking the Church to its core.

The "priestly" caste of *Montreal Main* is queer, not straight, and their religion is "anything goes," until, that is, they encounter Frank and Johnny. The film is fascinating in the way it positions the queer community as participants in the moralizing of man-boy relationships as it discovers an increasingly articulate language of critique. This is ultimately prophetic: boy love was emerging as a partner in gay politics in the early 1970s, but the LGBTQ community would later be avid participants in its destruction. The broad backlash against relationships like Frank and Johnny's would provide the gay movement with its reasonable limit—"between consenting adults"—the rule of thumb underwriting much of the legal and cultural gains of gay identity, permitting it to discard a political albatross and consign hundreds of thousands of previously gay men back to the closet.

And yet this anticipated trajectory is disturbed when we consider the creative process of *Montreal Main*. In this respect, the film and the video pre-shoot bear comparison, for the latter issues its own nuance, even if it is not as polished. Of special interest to us now is its vantage on the limits that the creative collective considered pushing in developing its themes. By today's standards, the film presents a reckless subculture, open to intergenerational flirtations. The video, on the other hand, explodes with speculations dangerous and shocking to all but the most jaded Internet users. In an extended shot, whose later parallel celluloid equivalent we find cut into only a few choice moments in the film, the characters sit together in the loft and rap about Frank and Chris (the boy's fictional name in the video pre-shoot). Steve declares: "You shoulda balled his little ass off, Frank ... You just have to touch him. Just put your hand on his knee, man, he'll get the message ... The kid fucking melts. Just stimulus sensory input and response. [He'll say,] 'I'm not queer,' but meanwhile he's all over you and is gonna be back for more ... They all come back for more." Frank can barely utter a denial, "I'm not in that league." If in the film he is overwhelmed by Steve's psychedelic critique, in the video pre-shoot Frank is terrorized by his enthusiasm—the nitty-gritty of a sexual encounter is somehow too much.

> Bozo: "You probably intimidated him up on the Mountain. When you say you touched him, you probably put your finger on a nerve."

> Steve: "The nerve was at the bottom of his hard-on, Bozo."

FIGURE 32. Video pre-shoot: The queer "chorus" Steve, Bozo, and Peter laugh at their ribald suggestions. DVD still, transfer from ½-inch original.

> Bozo: "You can't say hard-on to Frank. You can't say any of these words."

Frank shudders at Peter's innocent question, "I was just thinking, the thing is, can twelve-year old kids cum?" while someone suggests to Frank, "Ask him if it's clear or white." All Frank can muster is, "Jesus." He laughs nervously and offers no denials or confirmations or any theory of his own.

The queer chorus continues to give advice. When Frank

mentions that Chris (Johnny's name in the original script) doesn't have a girlfriend, Steve tells him how to make it, "You just say to him, 'Look, Chris, do you play with it at night?'—and that's your intro. And when he says yes, you say, 'Unbelievable, me too!' Then give him the secret handshake." The closest thing we get to moral outrage is Bozo's fear of Frank turning into Aschenbach "with a facelift, white vinyl shoes, a little rouge here, lips going like crazy." What's frightening isn't the idea of a sexual encounter, but the all-too powerful lure of ongoing deviance.

Fast-forward from the video pre-shoot to the film, and the fictional queers in this sequence have become responsible members of society. Steve is no longer aiding and abetting boy seduction, but is now a self-declared "Saint Laurent Street father figure" with "paternal instincts," saving Johnny from a creepy old man. Early in the film, in a snippet edited out of chronological order, Bozo sets the cynical atmosphere that Frank and Johnny's relationship will have to endure: "Frank doesn't want to have anything to do with Johnny, *per se*. All he wants is the rush of what it feels like to be a homo for an hour." Frank, along with the rest of the queer contingent, is an experimenter—with drugs, gender, sexuality, etc.—but he is accused at the outset of being a mere user of Johnny, a view the audience must grapple with throughout the film. Frank is not really into Johnny; he just wants another "rush," a drug reference reinforced by Steve at the end of the film: "... the same way heroin, let's say, or

FIGURE 33. My favorite arcade. © Rick Trembles, 2010

any other drug you use, will gratify a lust, right, for a certain pleasure at that time. But you have no other relationship with the heroin other than that which you create because it gratifies you."

The dialectic of electronic and celluloid versions of *Montreal Main* proves that boy love, then as now, emerges in discourse in extreme forms, swinging wildly between sexual excess and Puritanism. Frank is caught between the shocking experimental extremism of the pre-shoot—"If you wanted him to get into it, you could wrap your fingers around his neck"—and the soft moralism of those who only barely admit the possibility of an erotic friendship between Frank and Johnny before helping to squelch it. Frank's quiet, thoughtful manner gives Steve's loquacity the whole field of the argument. Frank, like Johnny, has no response. Steve, the voice of authority, speaks for both of them, granting Frank supposed "insight" into the essential sickness of his fascination and Johnny his "right" to be defended from the old men in the "tiled urinal of Babylon."

Steve nevertheless provides some wisdom to Frank and Johnny, warning the boy against the leeches on the Main and warning Frank about the illusions of desire. Steve reminds Frank that his relationship with Johnny has value because "at this time you have a relation, other than just that kind of gratification with Johnny." But it is only secure if he treats the erotic as "an illusion," keeping it "out of [Frank's] reach" or, as Peter puts it in the film, "make it an *esthétique*."

Steve introduces a memorable metaphor: "It's like you dig a butterfly when it's flying, right, you might dig it. But you don't want to pin it on your wall. You dug it when it was in the air, going from flower to flower. If you try to catch the kid, right, you're going to turn him into something other than that which you fell in love with."

Driven as it is by the reward of action—cumming—sex finds wisdom in hesitation, as desire entangles a person in the broader situation and in subtler pleasures than pumping and grinding: a name and a face, personality and dreams, a person's past and future, their family and friends, their interests, their way. Sex opens up a world of importance to us, and its demands sometimes close our eyes. The butterfly of Steve's metaphor is not only a symbol of vulnerability, though that is the focus of his argument. It also points to an appreciation for pleasures of other kinds, its iridescent wings opening in the sun, going "flower to flower," which would be obscured by the will to capture and contain.

Give Frank a blank check on his desire, let him think he's entitled to it, and he may empty Johnny's account. That is the error of a purely libertarian view of intergenerational relationships. It ignores the profound drive of sexuality as it seeks to gratify itself and posits the players as universally and equally desiring beings, thereby disrespecting important differences between man and boy. Frank's cock needs the barrier of his friend's caution to maintain distance between himself and Johnny, a space of friendship and respect where

Johnny can engage Frank, sexually or otherwise, on his own terms. Frank shouldn't learn whether Johnny cums clear or white because his friends are curious, but because Johnny is curious.[33] And if the boy is not curious? Perhaps boy love should be mainly a masturbatory pursuit, by far more looking than touching.

Although value can be rung from Steve's advice, we ought to refrain from valorizing him as the voice of queer reason. Peter advises, "You gotta give him a lot of room, Frankie. You can't restrict a kid," yet Steve restricts Johnny with his curio cabinet of metaphors for the boy's passivity: Johnny as a butterfly, Johnny as vampire food, Johnny as a tabloid crime victim. Which of Steve's illusions about Johnny are true?— Is Johnny merely awaiting an initiatory touch for his own desire to be realized, or is the boy a pretty "butterfly," whose capture would be the end of him? And why does Steve get to decide? He treats Johnny as nothing but an audience for his witty *repartee* ("You read me, boys?"). Unable to discourse with silence—as the now-adult John Sutherland remembers, "What was there to say?" (2010)—Steve overwrites him and considers that communication.

---

33. A point those involved in online boy pornography networks would do well to think about. There is a perverse breakdown of the fragile nature of relations when an impetus to production is reinforced by social expectations developed on anonymous networks, as if the relation was for some faceless, masturbatory observer rather than the beloved in the here and now.

Ultimately, Steve simply disrespects Frank's relationship with Johnny, his sharp attacks in the film pushed to the extreme garishness of the headlines in his tabloid collection:

> Steve (pointing to a *Close Up* tabloid headline about mother slaying son): "This is the greatest fucking picture in the whole thing. That's the picture. That's what you should take, Frank. This is where Johnny's at. Hey?"

> Bozo: "Let's do a *Close Up* issue on Frank and Johnny."

> Steve: "Frank and Johnny, right. 'Boy Slain,' right? Johnny in the bushes ..."

Duly inspired by Steve's spite and his breakup with Jackie, Bozo steals Johnny away from Frank during the outing to Lachute, mocking Frank, and proving that Johnny can't defend him from the hostile forces swirling around the friendship. Unaware of the implications of Bozo's nastiness, Johnny returns to Frank for the late-night return home and the beginning of the film's final confrontations.

Theater of suspicion
Joining with the moral preachers are suspicion and rumor—which animate reaction and produce aggressive behavior—justified as defensive measures against a public enemy fought

FIGURE 34. Theater of suspicion: Ann Sutherland gently cross-examining her son. DVD still.

on very private turf. Ann Sutherland suspects Frank and Johnny's relationship:

> Ann: "What have you two been doing down there, anyway? Do you go out places, or do you just stay there? … You must be doing something interesting, or you wouldn't want to go down there so often."

> Johnny: "Fooling around."

> Ann: "Fooling around with what? John."

> Johnny mumbles.

> Ann: "Fooling around with what?"

David, on the other hand, is shown pacing and unhappy whenever John shows up late. We gain insight by returning to the video pre-shoot. There, David specifically asks Jackie whether Frank or Bozo is gay.

But *Montreal Main* is not a deeply suspicious film, which is partly why it attracts our attention. Yes, the Sutherlands question the relationship and ultimately scuttle it, but the film is not trapped in a claustrophobic drama of fear, the way later films usually treat the subject. I would like to say the film is more successful by keeping it muted, but the times were more muted. The ever-present fear hadn't yet been made widespread and sharpened by constant, one-sided media portrayals. In the early 1970s, these were private fears, not public ones.

L'Argent de poche (*Small Change*, François Truffaut, 1976) depicts the child abuse narrative before it gradually became fundamentally "child sexual abuse" in the public mind—in continental Europe a little later than in North America—with the specter of the pedophile rising up as a new public enemy. The film is set in a bucolic French town where toddlers chase behind their older siblings and race unsupervised through the streets. A twelve-year-old boy gets into trouble, and his male teacher tries to discover why. He reasons that the boy's bad behavior is the result of parental abuse and negligence, which is solved by an intervention. The town is not gripped by the terror of child abuse. The townsfolk come together to right a wrong and improve a poor boy's life, not to fight evil. The one responsible for the boy's troubles, his mother, is not demonized, even if she is reduced in the film to a caricature.

In *Abuse*, which may be the last film with a positive take on intergenerational sexuality shaped from a recognizably gay political perspective, Larry, an openly gay, thirtysomething master's student making a film on child abuse, discovers Thomas, a thirteen-year-old boy suffering at the hands of his parents, and decides to put him in his film. They come out to one another, fall in love, and even have sex. When Thomas fails to show up for a date, Larry gets spooked and asks his doctor friend to check if he's in the hospital. The doctor says: "I think you're exploiting that kid. I think you dragged him into your homosexual fantasy world." *Abuse* is a great counterpart to *Small Change* because it reveals the heightened rhetoric surrounding child abuse, and the emergence of sexual abuse as the central pivot of the whole discussion. The tables turned, the one championing the abuse narrative is himself threatened by it.

In *Montreal Main*, the concern is private; in *Small Change*, communal; in *Abuse*, panicked. Today, it is an essential part of the fabric of public life in the West, and every case is defined as a public calamity. Child sexual abuse has gradually come to serve as one of the archetypal public calamities, alongside terrorism. Nothing has more power to incite parental anxieties. Sensationalized, these stories saturate western media whenever and wherever they occur, leaving the public unable to escape an inflamed sense of threat. This profound anxiety is generalized to all forms of intergenerational sexuality. An enormous diversity of activities, experiences, and contexts are reduced to simplifications that enable the unthinking interference that, in turn, lead to the destruction of the relationship.

Worth mentioning are two more recent queer cinematic interventions into the panic. In *The Nature of Nicholas* (Jeff Erbach, 2002), the panic is objectified as a literal transformation of the desiring subjects when a kiss between two twelve-year-old boys turns one (David Turnbull) into a zombie who blames the guilt-ridden Nicholas (Jeff Sutton) as the originator of the disease of desire. In *Wild Tigers I Have Known* (Cam Archer, 2006), the young protagonist makes a fumbling attempt to bed an older teen. His desires unfold before a backdrop of social panic, this time embodied by mountain lions said to be loitering around the school, attacking kids: "There's a lion on the campus. Please find a safe place!" Logan wonders whether it's true: "I think they're not as bad as we think. We're just told to be afraid of them. I mean, it's not like we've ever faced them or ever seen them, so how can we really know? It's like if it has a name and a face, we can hate it. And it's just not fair, so I don't hate them, and I don't think they hate us. They're just lost. They want to be here as much as we do." In both cases, the social panic is made material and open to inspection. But these queer interventions into the panic are, we must admit, quiet voices, exceptions to the rule of fear. Perhaps these voices will accumulate over time?

Hearts in Atlantis (Scott Hicks, 2001), set in the 1950s, explores the new order of suspicion well. A psychic on the run from agents of the American government, Ted (Anthony Hopkins), comes to stay with single working mother Liz and her ten-year-old son Bobby (Anton Yelchin) in an idyllic town. When Ted befriends Bobby and offers to pay him a dollar a week to read the newspaper, Liz feels something doesn't make sense: "Why would a man his age want to spend that much time with a kid?" She tries to communicate her concern to Bobby, but can't say the words, or let out the secret.

Liz: "Bobby, does he ... ?"

Bobby: "What?"

Liz: "Nothing. Promise me you'll tell me if anything unusual happens, all right?"

Ted is paranoid about being followed and directs Bobby to keep his eyes open for the "low men ... fellows who are ruthless and stop at nothing to get what they want." When posters go up throughout the town asking, "Have you seen anything strange?"—we are reminded of campaigns of harassment of sex offenders and targets of vigilantes—young Bobby rushes to tear them all down.

Bobby: "Ted, well, I know the Low men don't exist. But if … the strange signs appearing on telephone poles—well, we both know that can't happen—but if it did, would you have to go away?"

Ted: "Yeah, it wouldn't be safe for me, kiddo, and wishing cannot make it so."

The slow drip of motherly questions, and the mysterious past and dangerous pursuers of Ted, hover above the fog of fifties nostalgia. Eventually, the pieces of the puzzle begin to fall into place for the forces conspiring to capture Ted. Liz can't help but jump to conclusions when she comes upon Ted setting the broken arm of Bobby's friend:

Liz: "What the hell is going on in here?! … God, take your hands off that little girl, you bastard …"

Bobby: "Mom, no! He didn't hurt her! I found her in the park, and I brought her here so Ted could help her!"

Liz: "Go to your room! And you, filthy old man, you are going to jail! … Why's her blouse open?"

Paranoia forces Bobby's mother to choose the worst of the possible scenarios, her maternal fury overcoming all objections.

The Man Without a Face (Mel Gibson, 1993) portrays Charles, a fatherless boy, coming of age through his secret relationship with McLeod, an outcast with a dark past, who helps the boy study over the summer for boarding school entrance exams. The film version mutes the 1972 source novel's theme of latent eroticism and develops the dynamics of suspicion.[34] When the film was made in 1993, child sexual abuse paranoia was firmly implanted in the public mind. McLeod, burned on half his body, is called "Hamburger Head" by Charles's sister, and an object of public discourse, ridicule, and suspicion, a vague shadow with a mythic past— variably a freak, murderer, pornographer, and homosexual of whom it is said, "Nobody lives like that unless they've got history." Charles avoids telling his mother about his relationship with McLeod because, as his younger sister Meg puts it, "She thinks he's a psycho." The truth slowly spills out through Charles's circle of friends, and the boy accidentally reveals McLeod's secret: he was burned in a car accident in which a pupil of his was killed. The truth does not out, but simply raises the stakes.

When Charles runs to McLeod for emotional support

---

34. In the novel *The Man Without a Face* (Lippincott, 1972), written by lesbian author Isabella Holland, pederastic pedagogue McLeod is more ambiguous than the film version. He is never suspected of mishandling Charles, nor is he bothered much by the community: as for interest in the boys he teaches, he affirms simply, "I've known what I was for a long time" (149). Instead, Charles carries the weight of sexual difference, being curious about McLeod, who in turn grows to deeply love the boy.

and fails to return home one night, the police chief arrives at McLeod's door the next morning. He gets an eyeful when the boy comes down the stairs in his underwear, initiating the dénouement of suspicion and investigation of the boy's "best friend." Charles' mother, Catherine, probes her son for the truth of his relationship with McLeod. A teary-eyed Charles admits to the friendship, explaining, "See, he's my tutor. But he's also my friend. I can tell him anything." Catherine is panicked by the threat of sex, but doesn't want to say the word.

> Catherine: "Last night, did he ... or at any other time, did he touch you?"

> Charles: "Yeah, sure."

> Catherine: "How did he touch you?"

> Charles: "Why are you asking me this? I told you he's my friend, didn't I?"

In Catherine's mind, the possibility of friendship is obliterated by the looming threat of sex with McLeod. Her son's opinion of McLeod no longer counts because the "truth" of McLeod has come out:

> Catherine: "He went to prison for three years. The boy that was killed was a pupil of his. He was in the car with McLeod and they were having—he was

abusing the boy, Charles! Do you understand what that means?"

Charles, tearing up: "No. No. You don't want me to love anyone else, so you hate him."

Although his mother believes she is acting for the good of her son, Charles rejects this protectiveness out of his love for McLeod and doubts his mother's motivations. Rebuffed by her son, Catherine goes haywire when McLeod shows up and denies he's done anything to Charles:

Catherine: "What? You expect me to believe that coming from you? How do they let people like you walk around?"

McLeod: "You're being irrational. Let me—"

Catherine: "What? You want to see irrational? Mess with my kids, I'll show you irrational. Get out! Get out!"

In *Montreal Main*, it is the father of the boy who exhibits violent outbursts, attacking first his own son, then Frank in his loft. Fighting in the car, Johnny denies his father's accusations: "You've been in a lot of trouble since you've seen Frank." The audience may wonder whether Johnny's behavior is an effect of Frank's presence in his life or if Johnny is becoming his own person, with a will of his own, which doesn't always conform to his parent's expectations? Johnny is right to question his father's accusations because David won't raise with his son the subject at the heart of the matter: sex. Instead, his concern is displaced through other likely targets.

David: "Lookit, Frank is a lot older than you ..."

Johnny: "So what!? ... are you prejudiced? You don't want me to hang out with ..."

David: "Lookit, John! Don't see him, okay?"

Johnny: "If it's not you, you don't even care."

David, hitting Johnny: "Don't talk to me like that!"

Johnny, getting out of the car: "You stupid pig!"

David, at last, manages to get out of Johnny what Steve couldn't ("You're friends, aren't you?"), an indication of his desire to remain friends with Frank—but how much is Johnny's desire for Frank a defiant response to parental disapproval? Johnny doesn't understand how the age difference challenges his father, and he doesn't know how to negotiate his concern. To him, it's just "prejudice," a groundless bias. Johnny bristles at his father's executive control, which erupts in violence, an act that cements the independence of his will as the film closes.

The main confrontation between David and Frank is sedate by comparison, and especially by today's standards. David thanks Frank for coming down and offers him coffee and a cigarette.

> David: "I've decided I'm going to ask you not to see Johnny anymore."

> Frank: "Stop seeing him?"

> David: "I mean, a complete cutoff. It's got to. That's all there is to it."

> Frank: "Just stop. Wh— how come? Why?"

> David: "Look, I don't have to justify it to you."

David doesn't owe either Johnny or Frank a real explanation. This is about parental authority, and once the parental mind has been made up, it is for others to obey. Then something incidental but ultimately telling happens. Frank, suggesting he deserves an explanation or another chance, says, "Well, I'm involved in it. I'm a human being, aren't I?" David says, "You're what?" There's something so prescient about Dave's honest mishearing, because today boy lovers and pedophiles are not considered to be human. There's something prescient about David's honest mishearing, because today, boy lovers and pedophiles are not necessarily considered fully human. (One critique of "human rights" is that they are made unavailable to precisely those groups who need it most.) Frank has no right to know, but David tells him anyway, "Yeah, look, I don't want it to seem a reflection on your character or anything you've done, because I just don't know what's going on between you and John. Um, it's just disturbing, the whole situation, and uh, I just decided—" There it is, the disturbing "reality" hovering over the friendship, spooking everyone. Was Johnny really getting in trouble, or was his father descending into fear about the relationship, amplifying every little thing as a sign of the worst? Whatever the case, Frank is bulldozed without a defense, confidence in his position, or any chance of making good.

A most striking contrast emerges from an almost identical sequence in *The Flavor of Corn*. Duilio kisses Lorenzo in the barn one night, and the pair are surprised by the presence of his stepmother, staring at them. The next day, Duilio's father asks to see Lorenzo, who anxiously demands to know why. "I don't understand why you give so many gifts, professor," says Duilio's father. "I ask myself, professor, why you like Duilio so much, and what you want from him. Yes, I know you also visit the other boys. But with mine you seem different. So ... that is the simple truth. I see that my son loves you more than he loves me." Duilio's father recognizes something David Sutherland does not. His son wants to be with the man. Duilio's father attempts to negotiate his own feelings along with those of Duilio, his wife, and Lorenzo. He views the situation as a site of multiple opinions and feelings, which must be weighed together.

Lorenzo: "You think I did something to your son, right?"

Father: "Don't say that."

Lorenzo: "But that's what your wife told you."

Father: "Yes, professor. That's what my wife thinks."

Lorenzo: "Does Duilio know?"

Father: "Well, he heard his mother and his grandmother talking, but he didn't understand what they were talking about."

Lorenzo: "That's what you think?"

Father: "Listen, professor, my son says we're just a bunch of peasants: me, my wife, his grandmother, and that we don't understand anything."

The class difference between Lorenzo and Duilio's father may be read by some as a power imbalance that neutralizes the good will of the exchange. They'll say that Duilio's father was compelled by his circumstances to tolerate Lorenzo in the same way that poor, working-class, African-American mother Mrs Miller tolerates Father Flynn in *Doubt* (John Patrick Shanley, 2008). When Sister Aloysius tries to explain that her son Donald (Joseph Foster) might be a victim of Father Flynn, Mrs Miller responds, "Whatever the problem is, Donald just has to make it till June … If [he] can graduate … he's got a better chance of getting into a good high school. And that would mean an opportunity at college." She, like Duilio's father, is a "peasant" and therefore stuck with what circumstance offers her and her family. But it isn't simply a matter of acquiescing to the power of the priests. Mrs Miller admits to knowing what's been going on: "Well, maybe some of them boys want to get caught! … I'm talking about the boy's nature now … One man is good to him. This priest. Then does the man have his reasons? Yes. Everybody does." Sister Aloysius is horrified and threatens to throw the boy out of school. But in a homophobic world, Mrs Miller sees Father Flynn as her queer son Donald's only ally.

Class difference doesn't necessarily negate the value of the friendship, as Mrs Miller knows. If someone needs Father Flynn, they need him. Likewise, Lorenzo has something to offer Duilio that his father cannot give—not only love of a certain kind, but education and opportunity beyond the fields. In *Montreal Main*, the class difference is reversed. The Sutherlands are middle-class and Frank is bohemian. He may have something to offer Johnny, but it isn't anything his parents think he needs or can't secure by other means. That is why he can dispose of Frank so easily, and partly why Duilio's father can't. He continues:

Father: "You can come visit us anytime. But I want
to feel he's mine at least for a little while more. I can

use the field work as an excuse, and you can think up
something so that I won't feel Duilio has forgotten
me. Give me this gift, professor."

Lorenzo: "It's not a question of gifts. Duilio ... is
yours."

Duilio's father neutralizes Lorenzo's own fear by acknowledging his own fleeting grasp on the boy, for which
Lorenzo can be enlisted as an ally. He recognizes Lorenzo as
a partner in his love of Duilio, which can be sustained even
in the face of his wife's suspicion. Lorenzo, for the moment,
accepts the deal. Frank, faced with an ultimatum, has nothing with which to negotiate.

Affirmation and betrayal

In the films we have been discussing, the promise of the relationship is sometimes betrayed, and sometimes not. At the
end of *You Are Not Alone*, there is a beautiful affirmation of
love, when the boarding school boys conspire to illustrate
the biblical edict to "Love others as you love yourself" with a
film presentation of Kim and Bo embracing and kissing. But
in *This Special Friendship*, Alexandre commits suicide when
he is fooled into thinking Georges has repudiated their relationship. In *Abuse*, Larry and Thomas run away when it's
clear no one can save Thomas from his parents, and nobody
supports their love affair. It is a happy ending in that respect,
if willfully idealistic. In *For a Lost Soldier*, Jeroen loses Walt

when the soldier is redeployed, never to be seen again. The cataclysmic ending of *Dreamspeaker* reunites the old man, the mute, and Peter in death. In *The Hideaway*, Funder, moved by Møv's loyalty, risks his life and freedom to save the boy from falling off a roof. Howie, in *L.I.E.*, is betrayed by circumstances when Big John is murdered by a former lover who felt used and abandoned by his adult lover.

In *Hearts in Atlantis*, a tearful Bobby chases after the car that steals away old Ted; they press their hands together through the glass of the side window—like a visitor and prisoner behind glass at a prison, and Ted says, "I wouldn't have missed a single minute of it, Bobby. Not a single minute! Not for the whole world, Bobby!" Ted affirms the danger of their encounter, but also his willingness and lack of regret, even though he had to pay the price of recapture. When Bobby returns home, he has a brutal fight with his mother:

> Liz: "I did it, I did it for you. It was for your own good."

> Bobby: "You lie ... I found a friend, a grownup friend of my own, and you know what? I loved him. You didn't just betray him. You betrayed both of us."

Betrayal can have more than one meaning. In *The Man Without a Face*, Charles runs away from his parents to confront McLeod about the truth of the car crash that scarred him for life.

Charles: "I want to know the truth! ... Why did you go to prison? ... The boy in the car, the boy that died, did you molest him?"

McLeod: "What do you think, Norstadt?"

Charles: "Stop playing the teacher here. Just tell me!"

Charles wants to be reassured by the simple answer, "No," but McLeod refuses ("I didn't spend all summer [with you] so you could cheat on this question"), pushing the boy to make up his own mind. "Think, Norstadt. Reason. Could I? Can you imagine me ever doing so?" Charles trusts McLeod in the end, and the two embrace for the last time.

These two rather heart-warming affirmations of friendship make us believe in man-boy friendships—that they could endure, in spite of all the pressure, and even the inevitable breakup. But what of *Montreal Main*? Beginning with his nighttime bike ride, Johnny emerges from his silence to become a fuller, more active and vocal character, his will made sharp through conflict with his father over Frank. He arrives at Frank's loft, at the end of the film, with visions of moving in and rebelling against his parents. I wonder how many boys have entertained fantasies of running away and moving in with a father they thought was better? Frank, however, resists:

Frank: "You're kidding, aren't you?"

Johnny: "Why?"

One critic points to this as the film's "genuinely tragic moment" because of Johnny's "inability to understand why his relationship with Frank is 'impossible'" (Auty 1978). This may be true, in a way, but Johnny is not responsible for the entire tragedy. Much has conspired to make the relationship impossible, and no one has told Johnny why, not even Frank. Everyone is terrified that Johnny might know and consider the friendship's erotic potentials—whether to accept or reject them—and that is why it is impossible.

Late in the film, Johnny is willing to take risks to maintain his relationship with Frank and rebel openly against his father. But rebels like Frank must be more circumspect. He knows he has little power once a father has made his final decision. The radical freedom enjoyed by his circle has hit its limit up against the parental power that threatens to send in the cops. Johnny cannot see past the level of paternal control—"I don't care about him"—and can't understand why Frank won't let him move in.

Frank abandons the relationship at the very point Johnny is willing to take risks to maintain it. Without social support, Johnny's return to Frank has no meaning, and Frank has no power to receive him. The pair fly off in opposite directions, the friendship unable to sustain its dynamic any longer. But the cowardice of Frank's confusion, without any clear principles or vision, leads him to betray Johnny's friendship by cruelly ditching him. This time the barb strikes—Johnny is

FIGURE 35. Frank abandons Johnny. DVD still.

aware—and he runs off, smashing his Cokes, ending up back at Frites dorées playing sullenly in the arcade well past his curfew.

Frank and Johnny are, like Lorenzo and Duilio, poised at the boundary that the boy is willing to cross but the adult is not, because of the fear society has placed deep in his heart. Both Frank and Lorenzo are flattened, defeated by their lack of courage. But is it cowardice to fear the repercussions of overwhelming social forces? Lorenzo betrays his own heart, and Frank betrays the boy. Some in the audience may ask "Did it have to end that way?" Others may be reassured.

Compare the final scene in *Shane* (George Stevens, 1953), in which the eponymous gunslinger clears out the bad guys in a gunfight, with young Joey looking on. When Shane emerges from the saloon, nine-year-old Joey gushes, "I knew you could Shane, I knew it. I knew it just as well as anything," expressing faith in Shane's power to set things right. When Shane tells Joey he has to leave town, the boy asks, "Why, Shane?"

Shane: "A man has to be what he is, Joey. Can't break the mould. I tried it, and it didn't work for me."

Joey: "We want you, Shane."

Shane: "There's no living with a killing. There's no going back from it. Right or wrong, it's a brand, and a brand sticks. There's no going back. Now you go run on home to your mother and tell her everything's all right … You go home to your mother and father and grow up to be strong, and straight. Joey, take care of them, both of them."

Having gestured toward the path he wants Joey to take in life, Shane rides off, with the boy calling out for him to come back. Shane breaks Joey's heart, but he doesn't betray him. What was Frank's excuse?

In speaking of *Shane*, we need briefly to revisit the intellectual and political betrayal of David Halperin, who helped established queer theory in 1990 by crudely caricaturing pederasty in his differentiation of contemporary western same-sex orientations from Athenian man-boy relations (Halperin 1990). In a later essay, he returns to the topic of pederasty, or really pedophilia, by addressing the movie

Shane (Halperin 2007). After positioning himself as a "professional corrupter of youth," an implausible claim for one wearing so many wreaths of institutional legitimacy—denunciations in the Michigan legislature notwithstanding[35]—Halperin claims that "every proper boy has to have at least two daddies," including a male outsider who initiates the "boy into the secrets of male authority" (151). Shane, "like all teachers," says Halperin, "is a social deviant" (159). And although "the relationship between Shane and Joey is not sexual, it is not exactly unerotic. After all, the entire movie is taken up with Joey's crush on Shane. Without the crush … the movie could not endow Shane's example with [its] charismatic power" (160). Evoking queer anthropologist Gilbert Herdt's notorious ethnographic book that was the cause célèbre of 1987, Halperin ventures, "Instead of orally consuming Shane's semen … like any decent [Sambian] 9-year-old, Joey becomes a man by ocularly consuming the visual spectacle of Shane's masculinity" (162).

While queer theoretical attention to pedagogy is much needed, it is not clear what Halperin is pulling off here. It is not establishing a gay norm: "I emphasize that the phenomenon I am describing pertains to heteronormative culture … Gay men don't worship their male teachers, for the most

---

35. As he recounts in his 2007 article, Halperin's 2003 course, "How to be Gay: Male Homosexuality and Initiation," at Michigan's elite, publicly funded university (University of Michigan, Ann Arbor), ignited familiar culture wars in the state.

part, much less do they desire them" (164). He is, instead, developing a way into thinking about the homo-sociality/ sexuality of heteronormative culture, which is present in the hero-worship and pedagogical relations between men and boys. Straight men have crushes on men, Halperin says, in ways gay men do not. In a round-about way, and without announcing his intentions, he has effaced his *One Hundred Years of Homosexuality* by reservedly positioning the boy as a queer desirer circulating around queer pedagogues.

Will the queer community and its theorizing save itself from the stigma of a profound betrayal by exploring the "queer child"? Will it be possible to conduct this exploration without addressing also the "queer pedophile"? Is it, frankly, too little, too late?

Remembering

> "The truth ... is so overwhelming that it must be denied."
> —Susan Clancy, *The Trauma Myth*

Although Bobby and Ted's relationship was abruptly and traumatically terminated in *Hearts in Atlantis*, as an adult the film shows that Bobby continued to value the fleeting friendship: "There was an enduring gift that he left me. What Ted did was open my eyes, and let the future in." This is similar to the ending of *The Man Without a Face*, when an older Charles describes the memory of his relationship with

FIGURE 36. *For a Lost Soldier*: Adult Jeroen and child Jeroen meet at the crossroads of memory. DVD still. © Roeland Kerbosch

McLeod as satisfying a need for a father figure, the absence in his life that was the real man without a face.

These are conveniently uncomplicated rejoinders to the catastrophes that surrounded the breakups. The suspicions, fear, and panic ebb in time, leaving happy memories and a feeling of completion, even in the loss.

For a Lost Soldier is launched by a meeting in which the young Jeroen asks his adult self: "Do you still remember me?" Does the adult remember the experiences of the child, his pleasures and pains, hopes and disappointments, his fear and trembling? Granted, the memory-machine of cinema shaved off the rough edges of the original autobiography: "He loosens his belt, picks up my hand and takes it inside his clothes. Why doesn't he leave me alone, can't he see how tired I am? Will it always be like this?" (van Dantzig 1986, 166). These troubling questions seem removed from the film's nostalgic sexual encounters, but the film does not betray the book. Jeroen as an adult writes, as if to Walt:

> You can't possibly have disappeared for good before
> we have looked each other in the eye just one
> more time, wondering together or perhaps smiling
> together as we reconsider our strange encounter …
> How simple it was then to walk up to you, to watch
> you move up and make room for me on that bench
> and to wait for the moment—and I felt sure the
> moment would come—when you would silently place
> your hand on my knee. (261)

The narrow frame of cinema allows us just a sliver of our often contradictory feelings to be made tangible in the gossamer of celluloid. We must choose what to remember.

Montreal Main keeps us safe, on the one hand, by never consummating the relationship between Frank and Johnny, and, on the other hand, it keeps us in danger because that reticence might hold us back from engaging the questions and challenges that circulate around the film. Can we remember the relationship of Frank and Johnny without remembering sexual abuse? And if we can't, can we remember it as anything other than sexual abuse? In the language of therapists and law enforcement, Frank was "grooming," i.e., using friendship rather than violence to get what he wanted from the boy.

Susan Clancy claims rather boldly: "Today victims need to hear the truth. This requires us all to highlight publicly the true dynamics of sexual abuse—to expose the painful reality that most victims care for and trust the perpetrator … that they are receiving love and attention, that it does not hurt and sometimes feels good, and that, for all these reasons, participation is common (2009, 145)."

And yet she, in a nod to the orthodoxy, refuses to consider the possibility that the "perpetrators" might care for and love their "victims." Although "what hurts most victims is not the experience itself but the meaning of the experience" (185), no meaning but a duly updated abuse narrative may apply. Frank may be a loser, but is he also an abuser? It's Johnny who insists, "But we were friends."

We are often forbidden from talking about complex relationships in a complex way. Why shouldn't we think of young people who had erotic relationships with adults as comprising their own category of queer, with their own history, issues, concerns, and needs; not as the "queer child," carrier of an abstract "polymorphously perverse" childhood of some theorists' obscure fancy, but the actually sexual—the boys who do. Gay and lesbian literature abounds with claims about the terrible effects of stigma and shame. It is not only the men in man-boy relationships who are stigmatized but the boys who enjoyed their friendships with their older friends before they "realized" what it "really meant." Why shouldn't young people who have "deviant" sex come to an awareness of themselves as outsiders carrying the weight of social stigma? That is exactly what many of them do feel.

In *A Super Natural Premiere* (1997), video maker Kevin Kelly overlaps clips of the premieres of the classic television programs of his childhood with voice-over memories of the childhood sexual experiences he had with his teen brother.

> It's been going on six or seven months, maybe a year.
> I guess I like it more than [he does]. Finally it's over.
> He tells me in confidence that my parents know,
> and it has to end. I agree, but say maybe we can do
> it somewhere else [...] As I grew older, I became
> excruciatingly conscious about how inappropriate my
> behavior had been. By the time I reached twenty, I
> thought about it every day and told myself, "It didn't
> happen. It didn't happen." It became like a mantra.
> Finally I met someone [who] gave me enough space
> to let it out. I realized it had been a lot of pleasure
> and intimacy. It was an adventure, fun, and he was my
> favorite.

If a boy lover—literally here, a boy lover—understands his or her attraction only in terms of a lofty idealism, should anyone be surprised if the real, often ambiguous, complicated, and sometimes painful experiences of boys should rest uneasily in their young minds? When a boy looks out to see what people like their (former) adult friend are doing, he finds the media saturated with horror stories, and his own experience takes on horrifying dimensions. Can boy lovers address the complexity of the relations they propose and bring confidence to the minds of their boy friends? Most importantly, can they address themselves to boys, and not to each other or to a hostile society—two groups that are essentially beside the point?

There can be no doubt about the great responsibility that rests on the shoulders of boy-lovers to make sense and to make good. But when they lack the resources to fulfill this responsibility—not only financial and institutional, but emotional and social—who can say that they have not lived up to their responsibilities? "Pedophiles" have become targets of collective punishment—each individually held responsible for the supposed crimes of their type—without enjoying any rights to collective existence. Is that the aim of society?

The passage of time has become a vice in which experiments such as those taken by Vitale crack under pressure. And everyone is terrified, even the filmmakers. Greg Araki, the director of *Mysterious Skin*, admitted in an interview that he intentionally obscured the film's meaning from his two young actors, giving them alternate explanations for their actions and used creative editing to get the scenes he wanted (Ronge 2004). The condemnation of child abuse has migrated from an activity (sex) to its representation (pornography), to the representation of its representation (cinema).

(And also to the representation of the representation of the representation ... scholarly books such as this one?)

Montreal Main leaves us with Johnny being slowly swallowed up by the Main. The receding close-up on Johnny's face reminds us of the final close-up freeze-frame of that other canonical coming-of-age film *Les quatre cents coups* (*The 400 Blows*, François Truffaut, 1959) and leaves us with the same feeling: both runaway boys, having freed themselves, have discovered another boundary, this time the murk of intractable societal conflict. We ask ourselves what will become of Johnny, and what will he choose to remember decades later—friendship or betrayal?

The story of John Sutherland, the actor, took a turn for the worse shortly after the film was made, when he was badly hurt in a car accident in Europe. He lay in a hospital bed, unable to remember anything, a condition his mother the therapist relieved through her patient elicitation. Eventually, memories began to return to him, but nothing was ever the same (Sutherland 2009).

Sutherland's memory of the film was doubly distant; not only locked away in a time when he was thirteen years old, but trapped behind the catastrophe of the car accident. Even so, he has recalled this time with interest and a renewed appreciation, and the cinematic lens reinforces his memories of his parents when they were nearing middle age. He remembers his work on the film as something fun and interesting, when he contemplated being a movie star, though

FIGURE 37. Johnny and Frank after the release of *Montreal Main*, 1974. Production still. © New Cinema Enterprises/Photofest

he chose to turn down offers so he could focus on skiing and sports. When Frank Vitale came to Montreal in June of 2010 for "Montreal On Screen" at Concordia University to present his film, a person in the audience asked him what it was like meeting John Sutherland again after so many years. He said, "I was afraid. I wondered if I had screwed him up. It was a great relief for me that he wanted to meet and explore the film again." Johnny, as usual, said nothing and smiled.

We have written at length here on topics some readers may see as tangential but others will understand are essential to a discussion of this film. *Montreal Main* arrives with decades of heavy baggage. There is no short-hand introduction, no simple summary, except one that flippantly avoids the controversies, comes down simplistically on one side or the other, or perhaps, like Aschenbach, prays the baggage gets lost on another train, so the reader can return to a fantasy.

This chapter has called for a generosity of spirit, an openness to forgiveness, and a recognition of the many-sidedness of people and events. What is written here is an offering, not only for boy lovers and film lovers, LGBTQ-identifying people, or the curious and critical onlookers, but also and especially for Johnny and the loved and loving boys as well, who also live with the stigma of feeling different, abandoned, and silenced. We are thinking of you.

CONCLUSION

In this book, we have gently and admiringly dissected *Montreal Main* as a "queer film classic," thinking through its status, its form, and its various contexts as a *film* as well as its social, sexual, cultural, and political identities as *queer*. We have tried to do so both in relation to the rich and contradictory decade in which *Montreal Main* was made and in relation to meanings of "film" and "queer" that have accrued in the intervening history of almost four decades. We have analyzed the film as a product of a certain time and place and of a group of creative people in interaction with an art form in continuous evolution. We have parsed the film episode by episode and teased out an open range of meanings from its narrative impetus and meanderings, characters and discourses, iconography and sounds, its thematic undercurrents. Finally, we have situated this film not as an orphan kid but as a member of a large, transcultural, transhistorical family of kid films—of films about kids' sexualities and sexual relations with their peers and elders. This has led us to the enunciation of a twenty-first-century sexual politics for this 1974 film, a manifesto of the meaning of its intervention in today's broad international context.

In this brief conclusion we would like to come to the third term of the series rubric of "queer film classics," and think about the notion of "classic." In general, the term "classic"—

before it was hijacked, contaminated, and emptied by the glib marketing industry—implies an act of remembering and defining a work that, according to the *Concise Oxford English Dictionary*, has been "judged over a period of time to be of highest quality ... a work of art of recognized and established value." We have been remembering, judging, recognizing, and establishing the film's creators and personae, its dialogue with its historic and cultural contexts, its forms and textures and narrative arcs, its desires and pleasures, and what we have called its "intertext," or the generic galaxy of other works and political discourses along which it must be situated.

In closing we need to wonder who—other than ourselves—have done the judging, establishing, and recognizing. We need to briefly ponder the acts and agents of remembering that have ensured the preservation, re-circulation, and revaluation of this classic queer film. Together we are assembling and reinvigorating a collective memory of this film, legitimizing and extending its status as "classic." Rescuing this film from the archive into which it had almost disappeared involves active, not passive, remembering. The authors of this book have been helped in this by the living veterans of that long-ago summer when a "band" of film fanatics, Canadian nationalists, New Lefters, baby boomers, stoners, and queers got together with their grant applications, Portapaks, and Volkswagen van and started the video pre-shoot. By remembering fondly and nostalgically but also critically, selectively, and discontinuously, the veterans have been joined not only by the authors—two historians/scholars/critics/fans/fellow travelers/activists—but also by a small coterie of publicly funded preservers, restorers, and book publishers, and perhaps most importantly, by the diverse community of spectators and readers.

Who is this community? Who will continue to make it up in the present tense of reading this book and watching the DVD and, in the future, maintaining their active operation as audience members over the years and decades to come? More importantly, for this historical study, who has made up this community in the intervening decades since 1974? We have noted that immediately upon release, *Montreal Main* was welcomed not only by the conventional circle of distributors, critics and journalists, cinephiles, Canadian nationalists, civic boosters, and other cultural gatekeepers, but also by what we have called the "comintern gaydar," or underground circuit of word-of-mouth and shared subcultural communications that defined this film as "ours" from the very beginning. Within months of its premiere, Vitale had already shown the film to a major campus gay group and seen it programmed in proto-queer film programs in Los Angeles, San Francisco, and Montreal.

Thereafter, the momentum continued, with the flame no doubt fanned by continuous museum, festival and broadcast circulation extending into the early 1980s, and by the time *Montreal Main* made it to the influential San Francisco gay film festival in 1982, a revolution other than the sexual revolution was already underway: the home video revolution. The film had been sparked, as we have seen, by the introduction of half-inch video Portapaks, portable but semi-professional in design, and the National Film Board's application of the new medium to its community catalysis projects at Vidéographe and elsewhere. But it was the *really* portable half-inch VHS cassette, which was first marketed in 1977 and went on to dominate the home video market, that would sustain *Montreal Main*'s discreet career until the mid-nineties. The trickle of VHS copies of this film, taped off television in the early 1980s, and preciously guarded and shared, were soon joined by copies marketed by small specialty home videocassette firms that advertised in the gay press and catered to minority market niches. *Montreal Main*, along with many other titles produced before 2000 and mentioned in Chapter Four, though ever hovering on the edge of obscurity, reached the majority of its non-theatrical post-first-run audiences through these specialty mail-order exhibitors, such as Insider Video and Award Films. The vital mail-order underground traffic in photographs and films had sustained the homintern until Stonewall got a new lease on life among community networks marginalized by the mainstream gay magazines and media of the post-Stonewall decades, not only man-boy constituencies but also other "outer limit" constituencies founded on kink or

BDSM or inter-race—or even further "outer."[36] The steady underground buzz around *Montreal Main* eventually led, for example, to its presentation at a 1991 NAMBLA convention in the Boston area.

By the time of the consolidation of the Internet in the mid-nineties, minority subculture forums, networks, bulletin boards, blogospheres, etc. proliferated, enabling a lively virtual conversation about *Montreal Main*. The website *coming ofagemovies.com*, alongside *cvmc.net*, the first online video rental outlet (founded by the late "Brendan"), and *azov.com*, were all pioneers and continue to carry the torch. One website typical in its discreet nomenclature, *theskykid.com* offered an interview with Vitale to mark the restored DVD release of his film (Vitale 2009). The "conversation" continues to this day, stimulated qualitatively by the astounding capacity of the 'net as a platform not only for conversation and community but also for the sharing of pictures, excerpts, gossip, lore, and even integral works across the porous boundaries thought in 1974 to be impenetrable. One cannot be too utopian in the face of the ever-tightening climate of pervasive "family values." Yet the virtual community welcomed the 2009 DVD release of the film on *Montrealmain.com* with open cyber-arms, and this book will also, we hope, be in the heat of the action.

---

36. I am here using Gayle Rubin's concept of the "outer limits" of disreputable sexualities for the nth time. (Rubin [1982] 1993)

It is a sweet paradox that the kid film that opened with an image of Frank's loft above Cookie's Main Diner, 4318 Boulevard St-Laurent, and ended with a frame of Frites dorées, 1212 Boulevard St-Laurent, a film that opened with Frank dumping a relationship and closed with Johnny abandoned in those chill fall days in 1972, should have moved beyond this rich specificity of now and here and who, and entered into a sense of belonging with a global virtual community fanned by DVD, the Internet, cinephilia, and old-fashioned excited whispering across time, bodies, and space. What this means for the status of this modest, low-budget masterpiece—this charming kid film, *Montreal Main*—which we have invited you to adopt as queer, as film, and as classic, we now invite you, dear reader, to ponder ... and nourish.

REFERENCE LIST

Advice from the Main. 1974. *Transcript* (Sir George Williams University, Montreal). November 8–15: 3.

Allen, Luther A. 1998. L'aventure sexuelle clandestine: le cas du mont Royal. In *Sortir de l'ombre*. eds. Irène Demczuk and Frank W. Remiggi. 81–102. Montréal: VLB.

Andriette, Bill. 2007. Iran, Nigeria, Sudan, Saudi Arabia, ~~USA~~. *The Guide.* August. http://archive.guidemag.com/magcontent/invokemagcontent. cfm?ID=2F0C0DE2-C82E-47CD-B14592C4F8FFF244.

Angelides, Steven. 2004. Feminism, child sexual abuse, and the erasure of child sexuality. *GLQ: A Journal of Lesbian and Gay Studies* 10: 141–77.

Auty, Martin. 1978. Review of *Montreal Main*. *Monthly Film Bulletin* XLV(538): 222

Baxter, Brian. 1974. Review of *Montreal Main*. *The 18th London Film Festival Catalogue*.

Beard, David. 1974. An appreciation. *Cinema Canada* 11(13): 33.

Bennett, Rosemary. 2007. Hobby clubs affected by need for CRB checks. In *Falsely Accused Caregivers and Teachers (FACT)*. May 9. http://www. factuk.org/?s=Hobby+clubs+have+become+victims

Berlant, Lauren. 2004. Live sex acts (parental advisory: explicit material). In *Curiouser: On the queerness of children*, eds. Steven Bruhm and Natasha Hurley. 57–80. Minneapolis: University of Minnesota Press.

Birkin, Andrew. 2003. *J. M. Barrie and the lost boys: The real story behind Peter Pan*. New Haven: Yale University Press.

"BJS." 2007. 1 in 3 boys heavy porn users, study shows. *Science Blog.*

http://scienceblog.com/cms/1-in-3-boys-heavy-porn-users-study-shows-12663.html.

Brawley, Peter. 2007. *great fool of the fiery heart* (poems). Montreal: EberHAUS.

Bronski, Michael. 1979. Making sense of the seventies. *Gay Community News*, January 27, 13.

Burnett, Richard. 2010. An audience with Michel Tremblay. *Fugues*, February 19. http://fugues.com/main.cfm?l=fr&p=100_article&rubrique_id=90&article_id=14488.

Carr, Steven Alan. 2005. *L.I.E.*, the believer, and the sexuality of the Jewish boy. In *Where the boys are: Cinemas of masculinity and youth*, eds. Murray Pomerance and Frances Gateward. Detroit: Wayne State University Press.

Champagne, John. 1995. *The ethics of marginality*. Minneapolis: University of Minnesota Press.

Cinema Canada. 1974. Review of *Montreal Main*. 11(13): 32.

Clancy, Susan A. 2009. *The trauma myth: The truth about the sexual abuse of children—and its aftermath*. New York: Basic Books.

Copelann, Helen. 1974. Innocence sleaze and belly laffs. Review of *Montreal Main*. *Georgia Straight*. April 25–May 8.

Davies, Jon. 2007. Imagining integenerationality: Representation and rhetoric in the pedophile movie. *GLQ: A Journal of Lesbian and Gay Studies* 13 (2–3): 369-83.

———. 2009. *Trash*. Vancouver: Arsenal Pulp Press.

Dayman, Ron.1974. Review of *Montreal Main*. *The Body Politic*, November–December 16: 18.

Deleuze, Gilles, and Félix Guattari. 1986 [1975]. *Kafka: toward a minor literature*. Minneapolis: University of Minnesota Press.

Demczuk, Irène and Frank W. Remiggi. 1998. *Sortir de l'ombre*. Montreal: VLB.

N.E. [Natalie Edwards]. 1974. Review of *Montreal Main*. *Cinema Canada*. 11(15): 78–79.

Dyer, Richard. 1990. *Now you see it*. London: Routledge.

Edelman, Lee. 2008. Bad education: Keynote address. ACCUTE, Congress of the Humanities and Social Sciences, University of British Columbia, June 1.

———. 2004. *No future: queer theory and the death drive*. Durham: Duke University Press.

Engström, Christian. 2010. Urging MEPS to withdraw their written declaration. 29 signatures (blog). June 2. http://christianengstrom. wordpress.com/2010/06/02/urging-meps-to-withdraw-their-written-declaration-29-signatures/.

———. 2010. Written declaration 29, for data retention of internet searches (blog). May 31. http://christianengstrom.wordpress. com/2010/05/31/written-declaration-29-for-data-retention-of-internet-searches/.

Euvrard, Michel. 2006. Vitale, Frank. In *Le dictionnaire du cinéma québécois, quatrième édition*. eds Michel Coulombe and Marcel Jean. 737–38. Montréal: Boréal.

———. Review of *Montreal Main*. *Cinéma Québec*. 4(1): 45–46.

Evanchuck, P.M. 1974. Film and truth (interview with Frank Vitale). *Cinema Canada*. (September/October): 11–12.

Ferber, Lawrence. 1997. A tale of abuse. *The Front Page*, January 17, 21.

Fewster, Sean. 2009. Paedophile scout leader to stay anonymous. *The Advertiser* (Adelaide). October 29. http://www.adelaidenow.com.au/news/national/paedophile-scout-leader-to-stay-anonymous/story-e6frea8c-1225792448244.

Fidelman, Charlie. 2009. Study spoiled by scarcity of "porn virgins." *Montreal Gazette.* December 7. http://www.montrealgazette.com/life/Study%20spoiled%20scarcity%20porn%20virgins/2298048/story.html.

Finch, Mark. 1987. "Mala Noche." *Monthly Film Bulletin* 54(643): 245–46.

Foucault, Michel. 1986. Text/context of other space. *Diacritics* 16.1: 22–27.

Front homosexual d'action révolutionnaire. 1971. *FHAR. Rapport contre la normalité. Le Front Homosexuel d'Action Révolutionnaire rassemble des pièces de son dossier d'accusation. Simple révolte ou début d'une révolution?* Paris: Éditions Champ Libre.

Goldstein, Leigh. 2009. Documenting and denial: discourses of sexual self-exploitation. *Jump Cut: A Review of Contemporary Media* 51 (spring): 2.

Goodman, Paul. 1956. *Growing up absurd.* New York: Random House.

Gorrie, Peter. 1974. Newcomer has high hopes for first feature. *The Citizen* March 9: 61.

Greyson, John. 2009. *Montreal Main.* Unpublished manuscript, paper Presented to Winnipeg Film Group. November 1.

Halperin, David. 1990. *One hundred years of homosexuality: and other essays on Greek love.* London and New York: Routledge.

———. 2007. Deviant teaching. In *A companion to lesbian, gay, bisexual, transgender and queer studies.* eds. George E. Haggerty and Molly McGarry. 146–67. Hoboken NJ: Wiley.

Harcourt, Peter. 2002. *Montreal Main*: Uncertain identities. *Take One: Film & Television in Canada* 32 (July–August): 38–40.

Herdt, Gilbert. 1987. *The Sambia: Ritual and gender in New Guinea. (Case studies in cultural anthropology).* New York: Holt, Rinehart and Winston.

Hofsess, John. 1974. A plucky dance in the face of adversity. Review of *Montreal Main*. *Macleans*. May: 96.

———. 1987. *Inner views: Ten Canadian film-makers.* Toronto: McGraw-Hill Ryerson.

Holt, John. 1974. *Escape from childhood.* New York: Dutton.

Hubbard, Thomas K. 2000. *Greek love reconsidered.* New York: Wallace Hamilton Press.

Hughes, Polly Ross and Peggy Fikac. 2007. Legislators OK death for some pedophiles. *Houston Chronicle*, March 6.

Illich, Ivan. 1970. *Deschooling society.* New York: Harper & Row.

James, Geoffrey. 1974. On the fringe. *Time*. December 2.

Jay, Karla and Allen Young, eds. 1972. *Out of the closets: Voices of gay liberation.* New York: Douglas-Lynx.

Kapica, Jack. 1974. *Montreal Main*: A sensitive study. *The Gazette*. October 19: 48.

Kissel, Howard. Review of *Montreal Main*. *Women's Wear Daily*, March 8.

Klein, A.M. 1990 [1937–55]. *Complete poems.* Toronto: University of Toronto Press.

Koller, George. C., 1974. Canadian film symposium in Winnipeg. *Cinema Canada* 12 (February–March): 11.

Korczak, Janusz. 2007 [c.1919]. *Loving every child: Wisdom for parents.* Chapel Hill: Algonquin Books.

Kuhns, Williams. 1974. Review of *Montreal Main*. *Take One: Film and Television in Canada*. 4(4): 30–31.

Lasch, Christopher. 1978. The culture of narcissism: American life in an age of diminishing expectations. New York: Norton.

Lee, Betty. 1974. Bewildered film-makers wonder which way now. *The Globe and Mail*. February 9: 29.

Lee, Michael J. 2005. Gregg Araki and Scott Heim. *Radio Free Entertainment*, May 25. http://movies.radiofree.com/interviews/mysterio_gregg_araki_scott_heim.shtml.

Lehmann, Bob. 1974. Audience identification in a relationship film. *Filmmaker*. August.

L.H. 1974. Focus. *McGill News* (Winter): 29.

Maler, Mari. 1974. Straight woman meets Montréal main man Frank Vitale (interview). *Georgia Straight*, April 25–May 2.

Malina, Martin. 1974. Gay twilight demimonde captured in *Montreal Main*. Montréal Star.

Massé-Connolly, P.M. 1978. How to shoot a rubber gun. *Cinema Canada* 46 (April–May): 23–27.

Meiners, Erica. 2009. Never innocent: Feminist trouble with sex offender registries and protection in a prison nation. *Meridians: feminism, race, transnationalism* 9(2): 31–62.

Men advised not to approach lost children. In *FACT (Falsely Accused Caregivers and Teachers)*. July 26. http://www.factuk.org/?s=Men+advised+not+to+approach.

Michaelson, John. 1974. "Let's hear it for the documentation." About Frank Vitale's *Montreal Main*. Unpublished documentation package, including interview with Frank Vitale, Allan Moyle, et al.

Mole, David. 1979. Mainlining. *The Body Politic*, July: 33.

Monk, Katherine. 2001. *Weird sex & snowshoes: And other Canadian film phenomena*. Vancouver: Raincoast Books.

Morris, Peter. 1984. Frank Vitale. *The Film Companion*. Irwin: Toronto.

Moyle, Allan. 2010. Telephone interview with Thomas Waugh. April 21.

Namaste, Viviane K. 2005. *C'était du spectacle!: L'histoire des artistes transsexuelles à Montréal, 1955–1985*. Montréal: McGill-Queens University Press.

Nine-year-olds "performing sex acts in school." *Mail Online*. 2007. January 22. http://www.dailymail.co.uk/news/article-430579/Nine-year-olds-performing-sex-acts-school.html.

Ohi, Kevin. 2000. Molestation 101: Child abuse, homophobia, and *The Boys of St. Vincent*. GLQ: *A Journal of Lesbian and Gay Studies* 6: 195–248.

Orton, Chip. 1974. 'Montreal Main:' A lesson in honesty. *Manhattan East*: 4.

Perreault, Luc. 1974. De la 'Main' à Westmount. *La Presse, October* 19.

Perron, Luc-Alexandre. 2010. La gaité à la télévision québécoise. *Fugues*, March: 88–89.

Peter Brawley (blog forum obituary). 2006. http://mruttan.ca/mruttan.ca/blog/2006/10/peter-brawley.html.

Plummer, Ken. 2008. Studying sexualities for a better world? Ten years of *Sexualities*. *Sexualities 11 (February)*: 7–22.

Rayns, Tony. 2010. Review of *Montreal Main*. In *Time-out film guide*, ed. John Pym. 708. London: Universal House.

Refs "refuse handshake" over abuse fears. *East Anglian Times*. 2007. February 27. http://www.eadt.co.uk/news/refs_refuse_handshake_over_abuse_fears_1_79842.

Robe. 1974. Review of *Montreal Main*. *Variety*, February 27: 26.

Rodowick, D.N. 1997. *Gilles Deleuze's time machine*. Durham and London: Duke University Press.

Ronge, Barry. 2004. Interview: Under the *Mysterious Skin* (blog). http://www.ratherronge.co.za/html/sub_content.aspx?reviewid=198.

Rubin, Eric. 1974. Review of *Montreal Main*. *The Georgian* (Sir George Williams University), November 5.

Rubin, Gayle.1993 [1982]. Thinking sex: Notes for a radical theory of the politics of sexuality. In *The Gay and lesbian studies reader*. Henry Abelove, et al., eds., 3–44. New York and London: Routledge.

Russo, Vito. 1981. *The Celluloid Closet*. New York: Harper & Row.

Sandfort, Theo. 1987. Boys on their contacts with men: A study of sexually expressed friendships. Elmhurst, NY: Global Academic Publishers.

Schupp, Patrick. 1975. Review of *Montreal Main*. *Séquences* 79: 33–34.

Sedgwick, Eve Kosofsky. 1993. Queer performativity: Henry James's *Art of the Novel. GLQ: A Journal of Lesbian and Gay Studies* 1: 1–18.

———. 1993. *Tendencies*. Durham: Duke University Press.

Seymour, Stern. 1979. Film export and the new English Canadian cinema. *Film Culture* 58–59: 286–91.

Shatilla, Sandra. 1972. [Title unknown.] *The Montreal Star*, September 9.

Shewey, Don. 1980. Lives more interesting than movies. *Soho News*, June.

———. 1983. False grit. *The Village Voice*, July 12.

Shuster, Nat. 1974. *Montreal Main:* Gay's the way? Review of *Montreal Main*. *Motion*, March-May, 45-46.

Somers, Michelle. 1974. Homosexuality on Montreal's Main. *The Georgian* [date unknown]. Montreal: Sir George Williams University.

Stoller, James. 1974. Abandoning an androgynous muse. Review of
   Montreal Main. *The Village Voice*, May 16.

Taubin, Amy. 1990. Wild at heart. *The Village Voice*, August 28: 87, 92.

Tsang, Daniel, ed. 1981. *The Age taboo: Gay male sexuality, power and
   consent.* Boston: Alyson Publications.

Tsika, Noah. 2009. *Gods and Monsters.* Vancouver: Arsenal Pulp Press.

Tyler, Parker. 1972. *Screening the sexes: Homosexuality in the movies.* New
   York: Holt, Reinhart and Winston.

[Untitled article.] *Variety*. 1974. October 30.

Van Dantzig, Rudi. 1986. *Voor een verloren soldaat.* Amsterdam: Singel
   Pockets.

Véronneau, Pierre. 1988. Censure et discourse de la critique. In *Cinéma
   et sexualité*, Claude Chabot and Denise Pérusse, eds. 162–72. Quebec
   City: Prospec Inc.

Vitale, Frank. 2009. Interview with film director Frank Vitale. *theskykid*.
   August 5. http://www.theskykid.com/movies/interview-with-film-
   director-frank-vitale/.

Walsh, Michael. 1974. Review of *Montreal Main*. *The Province*, April 15.

Waugh, Thomas, Michael Brendan Baker, and Ezra Winton. 2010.
   *Challenge for change: Activist documentary at the national film board of
   Canada*. Montréal: McGill-Queens University Press.

———. 1981. "Nègres blancs, tapettes et `butch': images des lesbiennes et
   des gais dans le cinéma québécois." *Copie zéro*. October: 12–29.

———. 2006. *The romance of transgression in Canada: Queering sexualities,
   nations, cinemas*. Montréal: McGill-Queen's University Press.

———. 1998 [1993]. The third body: Patterns in the construction of the
   subject in gay male narrative film. In *Queer looks: Perspectives on lesbian &*

gay film and video. Martha Gever, John Greyson, and Pratibha Parmar, eds. 141–61. New York: Routledge.

———. 2011. What do heterosexual men want? or The [wandering] queer eye on the [straight] guy. In *Making It Like a Man*, Christine Ramsay, ed. [forthcoming]. Waterloo: Wilfrid Laurier University Press.

Wedman, Les. 1974. The low-budget principle. *The Vancouver Sun*, April 11.

Weiler, A.H., 1974. 'Montreal Main:' The offbeat life of 13-year-old boy. *The New York Times*, March 8.

White, Patricia. 2008. Lesbian minor cinema. *Screen*, 49: 4 (Winter): 410–25

Winsten, Archer. 1974. Whitney museum movie a hard look at Montreal. *New York Post*, March 8: 34.

Wittman, Carl. 1977. [1969]. A gay manifesto. In *Out of the closets: voices of gay liberation*. Karla Jay and Allen Young, eds. 330–42. New York: Jove Publications.

Youmans, Greg. 2009. *"Thank you Anita!" Gay and lesbian activist and experimental filmmaking of the late 1970s.* PhD dissertation. University of California, Santa Cruz.

FILMOGRAPHY

À tout prendre (*All Things Considered*), Claude Jutra, Canada, 1963, 99 min.

Abuse, Arthur J. Bressan Jr. USA, 1983, 94 min.

Les amitiés particulières (*This Special Friendship*), Jean Delannoy, France, 1964, 100 min.

Anche libero va bene (*Libero*) (*Along the Ridge*), Kim Rossi Stuart, Italy, 2006, 108 min.

Ang pagdadalaga ni Maximo Oliveros (*The Blossoming of Maximo Oliveros*), Auraeus Solito, Philippines, 2005, 105 min.

The Apprenticeship of Duddy Kravitz, Ted Kotcheff, Canada, 1974, 120 min.

L'Argent de poche, François Truffaut, France, 1976, 104 min.

Armee der Liebenden oder Revolte der Perversen (*Army of Lovers, or Revolt of the Perverts*), Rosa von Praunheim, West Germany, 1979, 107 min.

Ballast, Lance Hammer, USA, 2008, 96 min.

Barnens Ö (*Children's Island*), Kay Pollak, Sweden, 1980, 99 min.

Benny's Video, Michael Haneke, Austria, 1992, 105 min.

Breakfast with Scot, Laurie Lynd, Canada, 2005, 95 min.

Les Choristes, Christophe Barratier, France, 2004, 97 min.

Country Music, Montreal, Frank Vitale, Canada, 1971, 38 min.

Le Déclin de l'empire américain (*The Decline of the American Empire*), Denys Arcand, Canada, 1986, 101 min.

Le Dément du lac Jean-Jeunes (*The Madman of Jean-Jeunes Lake*), Claude Jutra, Canada, 1948, 40 min.

La discesa di Aclà a Floristella (*Aclà*), Aurelio Grimaldi, Italy, 1992, 86 min.

Don't Let the Angels Fall, George Kaczender, Canada, 1969, 99 min.

Dottie Gets Spanked, Todd Haynes, USA, 1993, 30 min.

Doubt, John Patrick Shanley, 2008, USA, 104 min.

Dreamspeaker, Claude Jutra, Canada, 1976, 75 min.

Du er ikke alene (You Are Not Alone), Ernst Johansen and Lasse Nielsen, Denmark, 1978, 90 min.

East End Hustle, Frank Vitale, Canada, 1976, 91 min.

Farewell My Concubine, Chen Kaige, China, 1993, 171 min.

Fido, Andrew Currie, 2006, Canada, 93 min.

Il fiore delle mille e una notte (Arabian Nights), Pier Paolo Pasolini, Italy, 1974, 130 min.

Fireworks, Kenneth Anger, USA, 1947, 20 min.

Forbidden Letters, Arthur J. Bressan Jr., USA, 1976, 70 min.

Genesis Children, Anthony Aikman, 1972, UK, 85 min.

Happiness, Todd Solondz, USA,1998, 93 min.

The Heart is Deceitful Above All Things, Asia Argento, USA, 2004, 98 min.

Hearts in Atlantis, Scott Hicks, USA, 2001, 101 min.

Hitch-Hiking (videotape), Frank Vitale (Vidéographe), Canada, 1972, 43 min.

Il était une fois dans l'Est (Once Upon a Time in the East), André Brassard, Canada, 1974, 101 min.

Joe, John G. Avildsen, USA, 1970, 107 min.

Just Pals, John Ford, USA, 1920, 50 min.

Katok i skripka (The Steamroller and the Violin), Andrei Tarkovsky, USSR, 1961, 46 min.

Kes, Kenneth Loach, UK, 1970, 110.

LA Plays Itself, Fred Halsted, USA, 1972, 55 min.

L.I.E., Michael Cuesta, USA, 2001, 97 min.

Låt den rätte komma in (Let the Right One in), Tomas Alfredson, Sweden, 2008, 115 min.

Léolo, Jean-Claude Lauzon, Canada, 1992, 107 min.

Lilies, John Greyson, Canada, 1996. 95 min.

Lolita, Stanley Kubrick, USA, 1962, 152 min.

Lord of the Flies, Peter Brook, UK, 1963, 92 min.

Lord of the Flies, Harry Hook, USA, 1990, 90 min.

M, Fritz Lang, Germany, 1931, 117 min.

Ma vie en rose, Alain Berliner, Belgium, 1997, 88 min.

Maladolescenza, Pier Luigi Murgia, Italy, 1977, 93 min.

La mala educación (Bad Education), Pedro Almodóvar, Spain, 2004, 106 min.

The Man Without a Face, Mel Gibson, USA, 1993.

A Married Couple, Allan King, Canada, 1969, 97 min.

Midnight Cowboy, John Schlesinger, USA, 1969, 113 min.

Møv og Funder (Hideaway), Niels Gråbøl, Denmark, 1993, 70 min.

Mon oncle, Jacques Tati, France, 1958, 117 min.

Montreal Main, Frank Vitale, Canada, 1974, 88 min.

Morte a Venezia (Death in Venice), Luchino Visconti, Italy, 1971, 130 min.

The Mourning Suit, Leonard Yakir, Canada, 1975, 90 min.

Mysterious Skin, Greg Araki, USA, 2004, 105 min.

Mystic River, Clint Eastwood, USA, 2003, 138 min.

The Nature of Nicholas, Jeff Erbach, Canada, 2002, 90 min.

New Waterford Girl, Allan Moyle, Canada, 1999, 97 min.

Novecento (1900), Bernardo Bertolucci, Italy, 1976, 315 min.

Nuovomondo (The Golden Door), Emanuele Crialese, Italy, 2006, 118 min.

Outrageous!, Richard Benner, Canada, 1977, 96 min.

Palindromes, Todd Solondz, USA, 2004, 100 min.

Paranoid Park, Gus Van Sant, USA, 2007, 85 min.

Pelle erobreren (Pelle the Conqueror), Bille August, Denmark, 1987, 157 min.

Peter Pan, P.J. Hogan, Australia/USA/UK, 2003, 113 min.

Pixote: A Lei do Mais Fraco, *(Pixote)* Hector Babenco, Brazil, 1981, 128 min.

Poison, Todd Haynes, USA, 1991, 85 min.

Pretty Baby, Louis Malle, USA, 1978, 110 min.

Private Lessons, Alan Myerson, USA, 1981, 87 min.

Pump Up the Volume, Allan Moyle, USA, 1990, 102 min.

Les quatre cents coups (The 400 Blows), François Truffaut, France, 1959, 99 min.

Ratcatcher, Lynne Ramsay, UK, 1999, 94 min.

The Recruiter, Adam Salky, USA, 2008.

Respiro, Emanuele Crialese, Italy, 2002, 95 min.

The Road, John Hillcoat, USA, 2009, 111 min.

Romulus, My Father, Richard Roxburgh, Australia, 2007, 104 min.

Rubber Gun, Allan Moyle, Canada, 1977, 86 min.

Salò o le 120 giornate di Sodoma (Salò, or the 120 Days of Sodom), Pier Paolo Pasolini, 1975, 116 min.

Sapore del grano (The Flavor of Corn), Gianni Da Campo, Italy, 1986, 93 min.

Scanners, David Cronenberg, Canada, 1981, 103 min.

Scorpio Rising, Kenneth Anger, USA, 1964, 28 min.

Second Best, Chris Menges, UK, 1994, 105 min.

Le Sexe des anges (The Sex of Angels), Lionel Soukaz, France, 1977, 40 min.

Shane, George Stevens, USA, 1953, 110 min.

Le Souffle au coeur (Murmur of the Heart), Louis Malle, France, 1971, 118 min.

A Super Natural Premiere, Kevin Kelly, Canada, 1997, 6 min.

This is England, Shane Meadows, UK, 2006, 101 min.

Ti kniver i hjertet (Cross My Heart and Hope to Die), Marius Holst, Norway, 1994, 96 min.

Times Square, Allan Moyle, USA, 1980, 111 min.

Tomato Kecchappu Kôtei (Emperor Tomato Ketchup), Shuji Terayama, Japaan, 1971, 72 min.

El Topo, Alejandro Jodorowsky, Mexico, 1970, 125 min.

Trash, Paul Morrissey, USA, 1970, 110 min.

Trevor, Peggy Rajski, USA, 1994, 23 min.

Uroki v kontse vesny (Lessons at the End of Spring), Oleg Kavun, USSR, 1989, 75 min.

A Very Serious Person, Charles Busch, USA, 2006, 95 min.

Vito e gli altri (Vito and the Others), Antonio Capuano, Italy, 1991, 83 min.

Voor een Verloren Soldaat (For a Lost Soldier), Roeland Kerbosch, Netherlands, 1992, 92 min.

Welcome to the Dollhouse, Todd Solondz, USA, 1995, 88 min.

Whole New Thing, Amnon Buchbinder, Canada, 2005, 92 min.

Wild Boys of the Road, William Wellman, USA, 1933, 68 min.

Wild Tigers I Have Known, Cam Archer, USA, 2006, 98 min.

The Woodsman, Nicole Kassell, USA, 2004, 87 min.

Zéro de conduite (Zero for Conduct), Jean Vigo, France, 1933, 41 min.

INDEX

Note: Page numbers for photographs in **bold**. Film character names in quotation marks and not inverted, e.g., "Frank," "Johnny."

About the authors

THOMAS WAUGH is the award-winning author of numerous books, including four for Arsenal Pulp Press: *Out/Lines*, *Lust Unearthed*, *Gay Art: A Historic Collection* (with Felix Lance Falkon), and *Comin' at Ya!* (with David Chapman). His other books include *Hard to Imagine*, *The Fruit Machine*, and *The Romance of Transgression in Canada*. He teaches film studies at Concordia University in Montreal, Canada, where he lives. He has taught and published widely on political discourses and sexual representation in film and video, on queer film and video, and has developed interdisciplinary research and teaching on AIDS. He is also the founder and coordinator of the program in Interdisciplinary Studies in Sexuality at Concordia.

JASON GARRISON lives in Canada.

SHANNON BELL is a performance philosopher who lives and writes philosophy-in-action. Her books include *Fast Feminism* (Autonomedia, 2010); Reading, *Writing and Rewriting the Prostitute Body* (Indiana University Press, 1994); *Whore Carnival* (Autonomedia,1995); *Bad Attitude/s on Trial* (University of Toronto Press co-authored, 1997); *New Socialisms* (Routledge), co-edited 2004. She is an associate professor in York University's Political Science department in Toronto, where she teaches modern and postcontemporary theory, cyberpolitics, postidentity politics, aesthetics and politics, violent philosophy, and fast feminism.

About the editors

MATTHEW HAYS is a Montreal-based critic, author, programmer and university instructor. He has been a film critic and reporter for the weekly *Montreal Mirror* since 1993. His first book, *The View from Here: Conversations with Gay and Lesbian Filmmakers* (Arsenal Pulp Press), was cited by *Quill & Quire* as one of the best books of 2007 and won a 2008 Lambda Literary Award. His articles have appeared in a broad range of publications, including *The Guardian*, *The Daily Beast*, *The Globe and Mail*, *The New York Times*, CBC Arts Online, *The Walrus*, *The Advocate*, *The Toronto Star*, *The International Herald Tribune*, *Cineaste*, *Cineaction*, *The Hollywood Reporter*, *Canadian Screenwriter*, *Xtra* and *fab*. He teaches courses in journalism, communication studies, and film studies at Concordia University, where he received his MA in communication studies in 2000.

THOMAS WAUGH is the award-winning author of numerous books, including four for Arsenal Pulp Press: *Out/Lines*, *Lust Unearthed*, *Gay Art: A Historic Collection* (with Felix Lance Falkon), and *Comin' at Ya!* (with David Chapman). His other books include *Hard to Imagine*, *The Fruit Machine*, and *The Romance of Transgression in Canada*. He teaches film studies at Concordia University in Montreal, Canada, where he lives. He has taught and published widely on political discourses and sexual representation in film and video, on queer film and video, and has developed interdisciplinary research and teaching on AIDS. He is also the founder and coordinator of the program in Interdisciplinary Studies in Sexuality at Concordia.

Titles in the Queer Film Classics series: